D0225861

Date Due

MAY 05 '95	DEC 13 '96	
NOV 20 1995	NOV 5 '97	
DEC 11 1995	DEC 2 '98	
	DEC 1 7 2003	
DEC 11 1995	MAY 19 '99	
DEC 15 1995	DEC 0 4 '99	
DEC 15 1995		
MAR 0 7 '96	MAY 4 2000	
	MAY 8 '97 DISCARDED	
APR 2 2 1996	DEC 1 6 '99 MAY 2 2001	
APR 2 6 '96	MAY 0 1 2012	
MAY 0 6 '96	DEC 6 2001	
OCT 3 0 '96		
NOV 0 8 '96	NOV 3 0 2003	
NOV 0 8 '96	NOV 2 9 2004	
DEC 0 2 '96 MAY 1 2 '98		

BRODART, CO.   Cat. No. 23-233-003   Printed in U.S.A.

Pro-Choice and Anti-Abortion

PRO-CHOICE AND ANTI-ABORTION

Constitutional Theory and Public Policy

James R. Bowers

 PRAEGER

Westport, Connecticut
London

LIBRARY

Pennsylvania College
of Technology

One College Avenue
Williamsport, PA 17701-5799

Library of Congress Cataloging-in-Publication Data

Bowers, James R.
    Pro-choice and anti-abortion : constitutional theory and public
policy / James R. Bowers.
       p.   cm.
    Includes bibliographical references (p.   ) and index.
    ISBN 0–275–94964–8 (alk. paper)
    1. Abortion—Law and legislation—United States. 2. Locke, John 1632–1704—
Contributions in constitutional law. 3. United States—Constitutional law—
Interpretation and construction. 4. Abortion—Government policy—United
States. I. Title.
    KF3771.B69 1994
    363.4′6—dc20   93–14739

British Library Cataloguing in Publication Data is available.

Copyright © 1994 by James R. Bowers

All rights reserved. No portion of this book may be
reproduced, by any process or technique, without the
express written consent of the publisher.

Library of Congress Catalog Card Number: 93–14739
ISBN: 0-275-94964-8

First published in 1994

Praeger Publishers, 88 Post Road West, Westport, CT 06881
An imprint of Greenwood Publishing Group, Inc.

Printed in the United States of America

The paper used in this book complies with the
Permanent Paper Standard issued by the National
Information Standards Organization (Z39.48-1984).

10 9 8 7 6 5 4 3 2 1

To my son, Dale, in whose life I see the future and become part of it; and to Gary Glenn, for being my intellectual compass on my journeys through the unfamiliar waters of political and constitutional theory and my own mind.

Contents

Preface

The idea for this book was conceived in the immediate aftermath of *Webster* v. *Reproductive Health Services* (106 L. Ed. 2d 410). At that time it appeared as if the ascending conservative excess, then dominating the abortion controversy, would harness enough forces within the Supreme Court and the state governments to overturn *Roe* v. *Wade* (93 S. Ct. 705), thereby severely restricting if not actually banning a woman's liberty interest in the abortion decision. In light of these seemingly impending circumstances, it became readily apparent that if this liberty interest were to survive it would be necessary to both reexamine the meaning of a woman's liberty interest in the abortion decision and develop a new middle perspective firmly rooted in the Constitution and the political theories informing it. This middle position could then stand as a constitutionally faithful alternative to the constitutionally infirmed pro-life and pro-choice approaches, then (and now) dominating the abortion debate. But in the immediate aftermath of the 1992 presidential election and the Supreme Court's refusal to review a lower court's overturning of a Guam statute criminalizing abortion, some commentators rushed to declare the end of the abortion debate and a victory for the pro-choice position. One syndicated columnist wrote:

> The great abortion debate is over. With the courts overturning a Guam law criminalizing abortion and the election of the down-the-line pro-choice president, November 20, 1992, marks the end of a 20-year abortion war. Never again will abortion be criminalized. . . . (Krauthammer 1992, 6a)

The general liberty interest in the abortion decision now may be more secure than during the 1980s, but announcing the abortion debate over is premature, and outright wrong. Even with congressional support of the Freedom of Choice Act, abortion policy largely remains an issue for state legislatures. And as long as there are opposing viewpoints on this issue, there always will be state abortion laws testing, pushing, and challenging a woman's liberty interest in abortion. Therefore, for quite some time to come, there will continue to be abortion laws requiring judicial intervention and clarification. For this reason alone, "abortion can be counted on to be the dominant family-related problem for the indefinite future" (Steiner 1983, 2). It will remain the paradigm and defining issue in any effort to structure a comprehensive and coherent family policy for the nation and the fifty individual states.

Though its intensity and focus may change, simply put, the public debate and disagreement over abortion is not going to go away just because the 1992 elections resulted in a Congress and a new president that are solidly pro-choice. Though only speculation at this writing it is probable that, rather than go away, the abortion debate will see the conservative excess of the past dozen years replaced by an equally unacceptable liberal excess. Thus, today state legislatures, other policy-makers, and the public still need a workable theoretical framework from which to approach the lingering and substantial questions surrounding the extent of a woman's liberty interest in the abortion decision and government regulation of it. This book sets forth such a perspective. It demonstrates to policy-makers how by being simultaneously pro-choice and anti-abortion they can address the liberty interest in abortion, the limits on this liberty, and government's regulation of it. It also explains why they must move toward this middle position synthesizing elements from the two current extremes.

In explaining why policy-makers must move abortion policy to the middle, this book develops a theoretical framework firmly rooted in this nation's constitutional reliance upon Lockean-styled liberalism. The book also argues that the Lockean-styled foundation of the Constitution settles for no less than this seemingly paradoxical position. In so doing, it provides substantial protection for a woman's liberty interest in abortion. At the same time, it balances this liberty interest against a viable fetal-being's liberty interest in preservation. This book further shows how this balance can be achieved and what it must entail.

In proposing a pro-choice and anti-abortion framework for abortion policy, this book challenges and assaults conventional thinking on abortion policy. Conventional thinking maintains that the choice in abortion laws must always be between the two extremes of a woman's liberty interest in the abortion decision or fetal life. Conventional thinking rejects any middle position recognizing the constitutional validity of both liberty interests and policy-makers' ability to find a balance between the two. The pro-choice and anti-abortion perspective presented in this book argues just the opposite.

By challenging abortion orthodoxy, the results and implications of the theoretical framework discussed in the forthcoming text will not satisfy everyone. In particular, the more strident pro-choice and anti-abortion advocates will find the framework presented in the following pages wanting. For in grounding it in Lockean-styled liberalism, this pro-choice and anti-abortion perspective rejects fundamental yet constitutionally indefensible arguments from both extreme positions. For example, the theoretical perspective proposed in this book rejects the more ardent pro-choice position that a woman has an absolute right to do with her body whatever she wishes. But the middle perspective developed here also rejects the pro-life claim that the fetal-being from the moment of conception is the same as a born child. Therefore, it additionally rejects that all abortion is murder. From the point of view presented in the following pages, these conventional arguments characterizing the abortion debate do not develop from and are not faithful to the nation's constitutional traditions. Therefore, these arguments cannot serve, and have wrongly served, as the basis for accepting or rejecting a liberty interest in the abortion decision. Thus lacking constitutional recognition, they cannot serve as the foundation upon which to build abortion policy.

In developing a middle theoretical perspective for abortion policy, the stated purpose of this book is to present a framework that is constitutionally superior to orthodox thinking on abortion policy. But in so doing, this book also underscores that *all* public policy, not just abortion, should be formulated from a clear understanding of constitutional theory articulating the limits on both protected liberty and government restrictions upon it. In short, an underlying premise upon which this book rests is that a constitutional level of analysis should be the starting and end point for the formulation and execution of all public policies. This form of analysis is concerned with the constitutional rules of politics "establishing the terms and conditions of governance" (Ostrom 1982, 237). As Lockean-styled liberalism long has been recognized as an original theory driving the Constitution's expression of liberty, policy-makers need to incorporate an awareness and understanding of this theory of government into all public policies likely to have an impact and impinge upon individual liberty.

The reference to "original theory" is important because it presents a third focus for this book. In laying out a middle theoretical perspective for abortion policy, this book is also about constitutional interpretation, specifically as it relates to finding correct meaning in the Constitution. It joins the debate over originalism by arguing that knowing and understanding the original intention of the framers requires, at least in part, a "jurisprudence of original theory." This means the dominant and prevailing political theories of the eighteenth century shaping the thinking of the framers need to be examined for what they reveal about the framers' intentions regarding the meaning of the Constitution.

In the case of John Locke and his impact upon the constitutional meaning of liberty, a jurisprudence of original theory requires that, once he is reasonably established as such, Locke must be recognized as one of the thinkers who had the most influence on the framers. Thus, his theory of government and liberty must be applied in any effort to find the meaning of those provisions of the Constitution in which his influence is likely to have been felt. Further, "whether or not a modern reader thinks Locke's theory is a sensible one" is immaterial (Tribe and Dorf 1991, 71). It, or the framers' adaption of it, must be relied upon. Contemporary political theories not present at the time of the drafting and ratification of the Constitution or evident in the framers' thinking are not to be relied upon or substituted.

By invoking this standard of original theory, feminist political theory, as a relatively recent contribution to political philosophy, is irrelevant in regard to finding the correct meaning of the Constitution. But so too is the far right religious dogma espoused by such ardent pro-lifers as Randall Terry or Pat Robertson. Contrary to the aim of these approaches to the abortion debate, the task of finding constitutional meaning through a jurisprudence of original theory is not to twist and distort the Constitution to fit contemporary values and preferred outcomes, but to discover the framers' values as reflected in the political theories informing their think-ing, to apply these values to contemporary constitutional issues through a process of logical reasoning, and to adapt contemporary values and out-comes to fit constitutional expectations (Tribe and Dorf 1991, 69). Properly used and employed, then, a jurisprudence of original theory becomes a fourth method of originalism, joining such established methods as textual-ism, intentionalism, and inference from structure and relationship (Brest 1990, 228-238).

ACKNOWLEDGEMENTS

A number of very special people lent their support and assistance throughout the writing of this book. Ummuhan "Sue" Turgut, a former student of mine, worked as an unpaid research assistant during the summer of 1991. She also served as a "sounding board" for the ideas expressed in a 1991 American Political Science Conference paper and a resulting University of Dayton Law Review article on which this book is based.

Mary Glenn, my original editor, deserves recognition. This is the second book on which Mary and I have worked together. Her "no fuss, no muss" style makes the horrendous tasks of writing and publishing actually pleasurable. As before, I thank her for seeing the value and merit in my work and encouraging me to pursue it. Jim Dunton, my editor at Praeger who brought this project to completion also deserves recognition.

Intellectually, I am indebted particularly to two individuals. Gary Glenn (no relation to Mary Glenn), associate professor of political science at Northern Illinois University, acted as one of my indispensable guides through the unchartered waters of John Locke's political philosophy and other writings. My intellectual debt to Dr. Glenn is evident in the dedication, a public recognition of my deep appreciation for his academic tutelage over the course of these past few years.

Tom Lindsay, associate professor of political science at University of Northern Iowa, was my other guide. A number of years ago, Tom was my nemesis in graduate school. Today, he is my good friend, and my intellectual debt to Tom is hard to describe. It is captured, in part, in the sometimes two-hour, long-distance telephone calls we had. During these late-night conversations, I would read Tom passages from chapter drafts or explore possible interpretations and applications of Locke's writings and teachings. He never failed to provide valuable assistance in clarifying my thinking and ideas.

My wife, Jan, also contributed to the successful completion of this book. As she has during all my projects, she tolerated my somewhat lessened but still present workaholic tendencies. She also read and edited the entire manuscript.

Finally, my son, Dale, is somewhat responsible for this book being written. In many ways, he has served as the sustained inspiration for my completion of it. He shares its dedication with Dr. Glenn.

Pro-Choice and Anti-Abortion

1

Reconciling the Irreconcilable

Fifty-four percent of all women who become pregnant each year in the United States neither intend nor want these pregnancies to occur. Forty-seven percent of these women, or about 1.6 million women, will choose to resolve their unintended or unwanted pregnancies through abortion (Gold 1990, 11). The reasons why they will choose abortion over birth will vary. Many of these women will not be ready for parenthood, and a child will change their lives. More than two-thirds of these women will choose abortion because of their inability to provide for a child. Reflecting the reality that a vast proportion of unwanted pregnancies also occurs among the youngest segment of women in their childbearing age, another substantial number of these women will choose abortion because they feel they are too young and too immature for parenthood (Gold 1990, 19).

Regardless of the reasons for these abortions, the fact that 1.6 million of them occur annually places the conflict of interests between women experiencing unwanted pregnancies and the fetal-beings at the center of a political controversy in which opposing viewpoints are so intensely held that one commentator refers to the abortion debate as "a clash of absolutes" (Tribe 1990). With equal conviction, both abortion opponents and abortion rights advocates pronounce the absolute correctness of their position. Both sides in the abortion controversy claim "we are pro, . . . and they are anti, anti-baby, anti-woman, anti-family, anti-choice, anti-life, anti-everything we and the country stand for" (Costa 1991, xi).

Indeed, "so intense is the moral controversy over abortion that partisans—both abortion liberals and abortion conservatives—are tempted, for rhetorical effect, to rely upon ill-considered arguments" (Cohen 1990, 567). Both opponents and proponents of abortion rights engage in a highly charged war of labels and semantics designed to inflame the public against the other side and to convince both the public and policy-makers of the correctness of their positions (Carlin, Jr., 1984, 65; Whitman 1990, 20). In this struggle for control and direction of abortion policy, "abortion activists now use every opportunity to repeat the code words that ignore their opponents' most powerful selling points and bolster their own" (Whitman 1990, 20).

At one end of the debate are the self-described pro-life advocates, those persons opposed to abortion. They assert the moral claim that the fetal-being "is no less human than its mother and, therefore, has an inalienable right to life" (National Issues Forum [NIF] 1990, 8). To them, abortion is immoral. It is also murder, and it must be stopped. Their impassioned rhetoric belies this deep conviction. For example, conservative syndicated columnist Cal Thomas writes that abortion rights provide women the opportunity to "kill off a substantial proportion of our next generation" (Taylor October 21, 1988, 1B). Similarly, in an April 3, 1991, letter to the editor of the Rochester, New York *Democrat and Chronicle*, one pro-life activist wrote: "It really strikes me as incredible that 300 Rochester-area women and men are going to be taking a bus trip to Washington to let the world know that they want to have the 'choice' to kill or not to kill the child in the womb."

At the other end of the abortion controversy are the self-described pro-choice advocates who support a woman's unconditional right to legal abortion. Equally as strident in their views, pro-choice advocates often begin from the normative premise that women have "a right to bodily self-determination" (Petchesky 1990, 3). That is to say, women must have absolute control over their bodies, particularly in regard to reproduction. For these persons, the civil rights and equality of women cannot be secured without their ability to control their reproductive process. Abortion rights, therefore, are frequently interpreted as the first line of defense against a sexist and unequal society (NIF 1990, 18).

The rhetoric of pro-choice advocates also speaks to how firmly they hold their position. Take, for instance, the uncompromising language of one pro-choice activist explaining why she and other abortion rights advocates from her community intended to participate in the April 1989 March for Women's Equality and Women's Lives in Washington, DC:

> We are making it clear that a woman's need to choose an abortion is basic and must not be denied. . . . We are marching to show that we know the real issue of abortion. It is not about "killing babies," as the anti-abortion movement wants us to believe. It is really about economics and power. What

better way to reverse recent progress toward equality than to keep women out of the workforce and in powerless "traditional" roles than by "limiting," in fact gradually eliminating, our right to terminate an unwanted or dangerous pregnancy. . . . We believe that it is morally wrong to deny us this need. (Moore March 27, 1989, 7A)

Or, consider the reaction of Kate Michelman, executive director of the National Abortion Rights Action League, to a 1990 Supreme Court decision upholding Minnesota's parental consent law. She noted that the Court's decision was just "another invitation to interfere in women's intensely personal decisions about abortion" (Whitman 1990, 20).

These polar positions are the voices most often heard the loudest in the abortion debate. They define both the terms on which abortion is debated and the acceptable range of policy responses to it. As the dominant voices in the controversy, both pro-life and pro-choice advocates pursue the incorporation of their points of view into public policy. But in so doing, both sides oversimplify the available policy responses to abortion by reducing the controversy to dichotomous choices between a woman's liberty and the fetal-being's life, and between criminalizing abortion or protecting its legality (Scott 1989, 319; Tribe 1990, 3).

Perceiving abortion as the "ultimate immorality," abortion opponents support the use of the government's coercive authority against it (Steiner 1983, 1). Their preferred abortion policy would be to see access to abortion completely forbidden, or at least nearly so. This could be accomplished through a Supreme Court decision overturning *Roe v. Wade* (410 U.S. 113), passage of the Human Life Amendment, or congressional action recognizing human life from the point of conception and the extension of Fourteenth Amendment protection to the fetal-being (NIF 1990, 14). Having failed thus far to make abortions completely forbidden, abortion opponents pursue a political strategy designed to greatly reduce access to abortion and related services. They advocate such restrictive actions as passing laws prohibiting abortion except when the mother's physical or mental life is at risk, requiring parental or spousal notification and consent, mandating waiting periods and informed consent, prohibiting the expenditures of public funds or use of public facilities to perform abortions, and promoting adoption as an alternative to abortion (NIF 1990, 14). All these actions are taken, pro-life advocates claim, to save the fetal-being's life.

In sharp contrast, pro-choice advocates interpret abortion as both a private choice and a private medical procedure. They assert that restricting access to abortion "does not belong on the governmental agenda any more than do other medical procedures that some deem especially unwise" (Steiner 1983, 1). Pro-choice advocates pursue continued constitutional or statutory protection of unrestricted access to legal abortion for whatever reason a woman feels is compelling. They also pursue an abortion policy that includes publicly funded abortion counseling and clinics, as well as requiring health care maintenance organizations and insurance companies to include the coverage of abortion as part of their regular services (NIF 1990, 24). All of these courses are pursued, so pro-choice advocates claim, to protect women's liberty and equality in American society.

For the most part, positing the abortion controversy in such stark and contrasting, yet simplistic, terms as the conventional pro-choice and pro-life positions do produces candidates and officeholders who take equally as unequivocal positions. This is particularly true since the 1989 Supreme Court ruling in *Webster* v. *Reproductive Health Services* (429 U.S. 490) allowing for greater state regulation and control of abortion. Today, a great number of politicians believe that they have no choice but to take an unequivocal position on abortion (Martz et al. 1989, 21). Take, for instance, the remarks George Bush made to the 1989 March for Life:

> I think the Supreme Court's decision in *Roe* vs. *Wade* was wrong and should be overturned. I think America needs a human life amendment. . . . I promise the president hears you and stands with you in a cause that must be won. (*Washington Post* January 24, 1989, 1A, 10A)

The dominance of the extreme positions in the abortion debate, coupled with politicians seeking their support, produce actual abortion policy that is equally as black and white. The stark differences in the Pennsylvania and Maryland abortion laws are illustrative. These laws clearly mirror the dominant polar positions in the abortion debate. The Pennsylvania anti-abortion statute, passed in the immediate aftermath of the *Webster* decision, prohibits all abortion except to save the life of the mother or to prevent serious impairment of her bodily health. In marked contrast, the Maryland abortion law is a modified freedom of choice act. It grants women unrestricted access to abortion up until the time at which the fetal-being is viable, or can survive outside the womb.

Reflecting the competing perspectives of pro-life and pro-choice activists, these two statutes suggest that abortion policy rarely seems to strive for some middle position or common ground between the two extremes. This is indeed unfortunate because many members of the general public find themselves in the middle on abortion. They accept neither the pro-life nor pro-choice positions in their entirety. Public opinion polls routinely document this tension in the public's thinking on abortion.

For example, a July 1989 *Newsweek* poll conducted by the Gallup Organization found that a solid 58 percent of the American public are opposed to the Supreme Court overturning *Roe* v. *Wade*. But this solid majority support for *Roe* is not a blanket public support for abortion on demand or a woman's unrestricted access to abortion. This same *Newsweek* poll also found that the public believes a woman's access to abortion should be legal only under certain circumstances (McDaniel 1989, 15). In addition, the public traditionally supports certain restrictions under which abortions can be performed. The *Newsweek* poll found that the general public overwhelmingly supports some form of parental consent and requiring women seeking abortions to be counseled on the dangers and alternatives to abortion (Salholz 1989, 20). Other polls also have found that while a majority of Americans believe abortion should be legal, many also believe that the government should neither support abortion services nor supply them to those who need them (Gold 1990, 50).

Perhaps the clearest evidence that the public is of two minds on abortion is the seemingly paradoxical opinion it holds on the morality and legality of abortion. When asked if abortion is the same as murder, half the public says yes. But more than 50 percent of the public still believes that women should have access to abortion (*Democrat & Chronicle* Editorial Board, October 7, 1988, 10A).

In short, most polling data seem to suggest that a large plurality of the American public is of two minds on abortion. Americans are both pro-choice and anti-abortion. This is true even for many self-described pro-choice advocates. For example, one study reports that more than two-fifths of the pro-choice advocates support legal abortion despite their belief that abortion is morally wrong (Scott 1989, 325).

That so many Americans belong to a "muddled-middle" position on abortion and find the issue difficult to resolve is not hard to understand. David Callahan, moral ethicist and co-founder of the Hastings Center, notes: "Both the sanctity of life viewpoint and the freedom of choice position are part of Western tradition. The reason that so many people feel [abortion] to be a difficult moral choice is because they carry within themselves both values" (Breu 1985, 91). But in carrying both values within themselves, those individuals in the "muddled-middle" know better than both extremes' voices in the abortion debate that the issue is "not funda-mentally a political question; [rather] it deals with people's deepest, most unconscious feelings about life, the power of creation, and the survival of our species. . . . They understand abortion and reproduction as both a private and a social phenomenon" (Kissling 1990, 181).

If a plurality, or possibly even a majority, of the American public is both pro-choice and anti-abortion, must abortion policy continue to re-flect the two polar positions of pro-life and pro-choice advocates? Is it possible for policy-makers to somehow blend together these two seemingly competing positions in a way that simultaneously respects a woman's private choice about how to resolve an unwanted or unintended pregnancy and the developing human life of the fetal-being, thus reflecting the sentiments of the middle group within American society? In short, can government create abortion policy that is both pro-choice and anti-abortion?

Some observers of the abortion controversy reject this possibility (i.e., Meilaender 1989). Others are more optimistic, encouraging, and cognizant of the need for compromise on the abortion issue (i.e., Callahan 1986; DeParle 1989; NIF 1990; Rhoden 1989; Rosenblatt 1992). Those who advance this third position recognize and accept abortion as "a tragic choice" between a woman's liberty or fetal life. Advocates of a middle position note that "precisely because there are two legitimate claims, it is essential not to sacrifice either of them entirely" (NIF 1990, 30). In trying to balance these competing interests, they support and pursue a political agenda that blends elements from both the pro-life and pro-choice positions. Pro-compromise advocates generally support laws permitting early abortion during which time the woman would be the sole judge as to whether or not to terminate her pregnancy through abortion. But they also are likely to support both government-sponsored alternatives to abortion and the regulation of it (NIF 1990, 32).

Though the middle or pro-compromise position has its adherents, in the rough and tumble world of abortion politics, it has not been successfully advanced as a serious alternative to either the pro-life or pro-choice perspective. Politically, the pro-compromise position is "reviled as unprincipled, gutless, wishy-washy, [and] apathetic" (Safire July 8, 1989, 27). Take, for instance, the official position on abortion adopted by the New York State Republican Party in its 1990 platform. The platform reaffirmed the Republican Party's "historic commitment to the right of privacy and reproductive rights" while it also maintained "strong and unwavering beliefs with respect to the sanctity of human life in all of its stages" (Craig and Del Prete 1990, 12). An additional problem with the pro-compromise position is that "politicians who otherwise enjoy a good straddle think of themselves guiltily as being indecisive when saying 'personally opposed but' on the abortion issue" (Safire July 8, 1989).

The pro-compromise position also has failed to play a major role in the abortion controversy and setting abortion policy because no specific well-organized and financed group advocates this position. Such groups as the National Right to Life Committee, with 1,800 local chapters, provide leadership and direction for pro-life advocates (Costa 1991, 171-172). Pro-choice advocates can turn to such groups as the National Abortion Rights Action League, the largest abortion rights organization with more than 350,000 members (Costa 1991, 166-67).

But a directory of abortion-related organizations list only one organization appearing to take a pro-compromise position. The Nurturing

Network, a collection of more than 7,000 volunteers spread across the fifty states, takes no position on either the morality or legality of abortion. According to its brochure, The Nurturing Network seeks to "discover the vast common ground that can nurture the seeds of mutual understanding" (Costa 1991, 174). Because of its neutral stance on the morality and legality of abortion, this group's focus is not on public policy. Instead, the Nurturing Network's primary emphasis is on meeting the needs of women facing unwanted and unintended pregnancies by providing these women with needed services (Costa 1991, 174). Built upon a recognition that for most middle class women the root cause of abortion has less to do with poverty than with the "conflict between motherhood and life plans," the Nurturing Network has organized a national network to "keep the client's life, and resumé, intact." (Mathews-Green 1991, 29).

Perhaps the greatest limitation of the pro-compromise position currently is the absence of a well-thought-out theoretical framework around which to organize and demonstrate to policy-makers how government can be both pro-choice and anti-abortion. This is not to say that the pro-compromise position is absent any foundation. It is not. As currently expressed, the theoretical underpinning of the pro-compromise position concentrates upon the social effects of the abortion controversy on the long-term interests of the community, particularly its impact on the social and political institutions on which the community's common life depends (NIF 1990, 28-31).

Recognizing the pluralistic nature of American society, proponents of the pro-compromise position accept that in a nation like the United States, "whose citizens share no common background, no common religion, and few common values—most matters of personal morality [like abortion] must be kept out of the public realm" (NIF 1990, 28-29). At the same time, though, the community's interest in potential life must be recognized and appreciated (NIF 1990, 32). Thus, the proper balance in abortion policy is one that recognizes a woman has a privacy interest in deciding how to resolve an unwanted pregnancy, though not an absolute one, and at the same time shows an increasing concern for the developing human life of the fetal-being as it approaches term (NIF 1990, 28-32).

The awareness of and sensitivity to both a woman's privacy interest and the developing human life of the fetal-being that the pro-compromise position brings to the abortion debate can serve as a middle ground for abortion policy that fosters government being both pro-choice and anti-abortion. But for the position to do so, a more fully developed theoretical framework capable of defining the limits of both the pro-choice and anti-abortion components of this policy must be devised. To clearly set these limits, the theoretical framework of the pro-compromise position must be faithful to this nation's constitutional heritage and the ideas that shaped it.

Recognition of pluralism and private morality points it in the right direction. But an even greater faithfulness can be achieved by applying the liberal teachings and writings of John Locke to the abortion controversy. This, in turn, provides a more convincing counterposition to either the pro-life or pro-choice position. Locke is essential to resolving the abortion controversy because, as Chapters 2 and 3 show, Lockean-styled political thought contributed mightily to shaping the political thinking of the nation's founding generation and the framers of the Constitution. In particular, Lockean-styled liberalism was the theory of individual rights informing both American independence from Great Britain and the Constitution of 1787. Therefore, in regard to individual liberty and the Constitution, Locke can be thought of as the original theoretician behind the thinking of the framers. Thus, to understand the framers' intent regarding liberty, it is first necessary to understand Locke's Liberalism. Locke's ideas can then be applied to the abortion controversy to ascertain the constitutionally correct nature of abortion policy. In so doing, "a *permanent* and *secure* place in American law for the right of women to make their own choice" regarding abortion can be achieved. As will be made clear in forthcoming discussions, it will be a place that allows for "a far richer and more sensitive notion of the nature of that choice" than the conventional pro-choice and pro-life positions can provide (Callahan 1990, 682).

The basic argument that unfolds in succeeding chapters is that, properly understood, Lockean-styled liberalism and, therefore, the Constitution require government to be both pro-choice and anti-abortion. Locke's liberalism prohibits government from interfering with individuals' choices made in the private sphere of their lives unless this interference is necessary to reaffirm natural rights. Procreation decisions, including the resolution of unwanted pregnancies by abortion, resides in this private sphere. Locating the abortion decision here effectively means government has no alternative but to be pro-choice in so far as pro-choice means prohibiting an outright ban on abortion or other governmental actions designed to coerce women into not having abortions. But as Chapter 4 discusses, a constitutional obligation to be pro-choice may mean little more than this. Thus, such standard abortion rights positions as public funding of abortions and related services for impoverished women are permissible but not constitutionally required. Continuing this discussion, Chapter 5 applies this Lockean understanding of pro-choice to minor women and their access to abortion.

If government has no constitutional alternative but to be pro-choice, how can it also be anti-abortion? First, though Locke's liberalism prohibits government from directly interfering with choices made in the private sphere, it allows government to use noncoercive means to try and influence these choices. In regard to abortion policy, government can choose to be anti-abortion by pursuing programs that encourage, give incentives to, or enable women experiencing unwanted pregnancies to choose parent-hood or adoption over abortion. Through this approach, government can function within the Constitution's tradition of Lockean-styled liberalism while still promoting its favored position on abortion.

Second, Locke's liberalism also reveals to government when it can and must use its coercive powers to be anti-abortion. As Chapter 6 dis-cusses more fully, the Lockean-styled nature of the Constitution accepts government restrictions on individual liberties at that point where those liberties are used in ways harmful to the individual's self-preservation or to others. In addition, as Chapter 6 also shows, Locke's teachings and writings provide an understanding of fetal-rights. It does so by supplying the criteria by which to judge at what point the fetal-being possesses personhood, thereby securing for itself some modicum of individual rights. On this matter, Locke also can be applied to a discussion of the obligation of the pregnant woman to the fetal-being, and government obligation to protect the fetal-being's developing liberty interests. Thus, when properly understood and applied, Lockean-styled liberalism de-fines the parameters of both the liberty interest in the abortion decision and acceptable abortion policy directed at this liberty interest. How this perspective can be applied to formulate and evaluate actual abortion policy can be illustrated through a Lockean-styled analysis of the Freedom of Choice Act introduced into both the 101 and 102 Congress. Chapter 7 conducts such an analysis.

2

An Introduction to John Locke's Liberalism

THE STATE OF NATURE

John Locke's liberalism is a natural rights theory of liberty and government. By natural rights, Locke can be understood to mean rights that are naturally possessed and not bestowed on individuals by some higher civil or political authority. Instead, these rights are discovered through reason by observing the natural relations among individuals (Lamprecht 1962, 122).

In asserting this claim of natural rights, Locke teaches that person-kind originally exists in a state of nature, a condition in which individuals live "together according to reason, without a common Superior on Earth, with Authority to judge between them" (*Second Treatise*, sec. 19). In this state of nature individuals enjoy perfect and total freedom to "order their actions, and dispose of their possessions and persons, as they think fit, within the bounds of the law of nature, without asking leave, or depending upon the will of any other man" (*Second Treatise*, sec. 4). In short, in a state of nature, an individual is totally nonsubordinate to any other individual (Diamond 1976, 316). Locke further teaches that this state of nature is also a state of perfect equality in which all individuals are born to "the same advantages of Nature and use of the same faculties" (*Second Treatise*, sec. 4). All individuals, therefore, enjoy the same liberty as others with "no one having more than another" (*Second Treatise*, sec. 4). The complete and equal liberty individuals possess in a state of nature is qualified in two important ways. First, when Locke writes that personkind's original condition is a state of nature, he does not mean that individuals exist outside of any society (McDonald 1985, 62). While they are autonomous beings, they do not live autonomous lives completely removed from interactions with other individuals. To the contrary, "Necessity, Convenience, and Inclination drives [individuals] into *Society*" (*Second Treatise*, sec. 77–emphasis in the original). The three societies found in a state of nature are those between husbands and wives, parents and children, and masters and servants (*Second Treatise*, secs. 77-87). To be in a state of nature, then, only means the individuals are under no common superior authority able to judge them; that is, they exist without the benefit of any civil or political society (Goldwin 1976, 128).

Second, freedom in a state of nature is not uncontrollable liberty or license "for every one to do what he lists, to live as he pleases, and not to be tied to any law" (*Second Treatise*, sec. 22). "Real liberty for all could not exist under the operation of a principle which recognized the right of each individual person to use his own [liberty] . . . regardless of the injury that may be done. . . ." (*Jacobson* v. *Massachusetts*, 197 U.S. 11, 26). Therefore, the state of nature, from which all liberty is derived, "has a Law of Nature to govern it, which obligates everyone" equally (*Second Treatise*, sec. 6).

For example, rising from the natural right of self-preservation, the law of nature obligates all individuals to preserve themselves and "not to quit [their] Station wilfully" (*Second Treatise*, sec. 6). In addition, the law of nature stipulates that "no one ought to harm another in his Life, Health, Liberty, or Possessions" (*Second Treatise*, sec. 6). Through this stipulation, the law of nature further obligates individuals to *preserve the rest of Mankind*" as much as they can when their own preservation is not put at risk by doing so (*Second Treatise*, sec. 6–emphasis in the original).

Though the law of nature places these and other constraints on individual behavior in a state of nature, some persons will choose not to live according to its dictates. By their actions, these individuals "declare [themselves] to live by another Rule, than that of *reason* and common Equity" (*Second Treatise*, sec. 8). Thus, to preserve themselves and the rest of personkind from those who do not live according to the law of nature, all individuals also have the natural powers to judge and punish those persons who offend it (*Second Treatise*, secs. 7-13). Like liberty, the powers to judge and punish are not absolute. The law of nature dictates that the powers to judge and punish transgressors against the law are limited to that "degree, and with so much *Severity* as will suffice to make it an ill bargain to the Offender[s], give [them] cause to repent, and terrify others from doing the like" (*Second Treatise*, sec. 12).

Second, the law of nature also recognizes that the general right to punish has component parts, one of which only the injured parties can pursue. All persons are able to punish transgressors of the law of nature in order to restrain the offenders and secure their repentance. But only the injured parties can punish for reparation. Locke writes that through the right of self-preservation, these persons have the power to appropriate for themselves "the Goods or Service of the Offender[s]" (*Second Treatise*, sec. 11).

The need to judge and punish transgressors of the law of nature reveals the darker side of residing in a state of nature. Though individuals may possess perfect freedom and equality in this state, this liberty is very unsafe and unsecured. It is open to constant invasion from those individuals willing to live outside the law of nature (*Second Treatise*, sec. 123).

This precarious state of liberty is compounded by the potential arbitrariness and ineffectiveness of the natural powers of judging and punishing. First, because of either self-interest or the lack of study of and reflection on the law of nature, individuals judging transgressions against their own liberty may refuse or fail to correctly apply nature's law. Therefore, in a state of nature, there is likely to be the absence of any known and settled law established "by common consent to be the Standard of Right and Wrong, and the common measure to decide all Controversies" (*Second Treatise*, sec. 124).

Second, in a state of nature there will likely be an absence of impartial judges dispensing fair punishment. Locke writes that individuals are "partial to themselves." When they act as their own judge and executioner against those who have transgressed their liberty, "passion and revenge are very apt to carry them too far, and with too much heat" (*Second Treatise*, sec. 125). Third, even if the other two imperfections in judging and punishing could be overcome, individuals in a state of nature, acting in isolation from one another, may not possess the power necessary to actually punish those who violated their liberty (*Second Treatise*, sec. 126).

Since in a state of nature, perfect freedom "is full of fear and continual dangers," and the process of judging and punishing risks being arbitrary and uncertain, individuals find it necessary to leave it and unite with others in a civil or political society for the purpose of preserving and better enjoying their "property," which Locke defines as their "Lives, Liberties, and Estates" (*Second Treatise*, sec. 124). Indeed, this desire to avoid and remedy the inconveniences found in a state of nature is the foundation on which all civil or political societies are built (*Second Treatise*, sec. 90). Thus, civil or political society appears to be the only alternative Locke sees for the uncertain state of nature (Lamprecht 1962, 131).

THE CIVIL SOCIETY

Personkind constitutes a civil or political society to procure, preserve, and advance their "civil interests," which Locke defines as "life, liberty, health, . . . indolence of body, and the possession of outward things, such as money, land, houses, furniture" (*A Letter concerning Toleration*,

9-10). In constituting a political society for these reasons, individuals do not lose liberty but, as it is discussed later, liberty is transformed. Rather, individuals transfer to the civil society only their natural powers to judge and punish (*Second Treatise*, sec. 128). In return, the newly formed political society remedies the uncertainties in the state of nature by providing to all individuals within the community known and settled laws, impartial judges, and power actually capable of executing punishment against those who fail to live by the community's laws (*Second Treatise*, secs. 87, 89, 124-126).

Transferring these powers to judge and punish from individuals to the political society occurs through consent. In fact, Locke teaches that consent is the only way that individuals can divest themselves from their "Natural Liberty" and put on "*the bonds of Civil Society*" (*Second Treatise*, sec. 95–emphasis in the original). These bonds of civil society, though they do not represent a loss of liberty, do change its nature:

> The *Natural Liberty* of man is to be free from any Superior Power on Earth, and not to be under the Will or Legislative Authority of Man, but to have only the Law of Nature for his Rule. The *Liberty of Man, in Society*, is to be under no other Legislative Power, but established by consent, . . . nor under the Dominion of any Will, or Restraint of any Law, but what the Legislative shall enact, according to the Trust put in it. (*Second Treatise*, sec. 22)

To be under only the legislative powers to which they consented means that individuals also consent to be under the "will and determination of the *majority*" within the civil society being established (*Second Treatise*, sec. 96–emphasis in the original). The end for which the civil society is created, i.e., securing liberty, necessitates this majority control. Locke writes: "Whosoever . . . out of a state of nature unite into a *Community*, must be understood to give up all the power necessary to the ends for which they unite into Society, to the *majority*" (*Second Treatise*, sec. 99–emphasis in the original). In this regard, majority control is a means to the end of civil society in that it enables the community to act as "one coherent living Body." Any numerical control greater than a simple majority would likely inhibit the civil society from acting in this way. Accordingly, Locke writes:

> For when any number of Men have . . . made a *Community*, they have thereby made that *Community* one Body, with a Power to Act as one Body. . . . [I]t being necessary to that which is one body to move one way; it is necessary the Body should move that way whither the greater force carries it, which is the *consent of the majority*. . . . For if *the consent of the majority* shall not in reason, be received as *the act of the whole* . . . nothing but the consent of every individual can make anything the act of the whole:

But such a consent is next to impossible ever to be had. . . . (*Second Treatise,* secs. 96-98–emphasis in the original)

For Locke, then, the legislature is *"the Soul that gives Form, Life, and Unity to the Commonwealth"* through which the society acts as one body (*Second Treatise*, sec. 212–emphasis in the original). Without this ability to act as one body, the legislature would be unable to provide known, settled, and impartially applied laws capable of securing the uncertain liberty found in a state of nature. If this condition were to exist, members of the civil society would be no better off than if they had remained in a state of nature (*Second Treatise*, sec. 97).

Locke clearly believes that reason requires all individuals to be bound to the civil laws enacted by the community's majority. But this obligation should not be overstated. Upon entering a political society, individuals do not trade the uncertainty of liberty in a state of nature for the absolute rule of a majority. The absolute or unrestrained power of the majority would be as great if not a greater threat to liberty than remaining in a state of nature. Such a condition would make it irrational to leave a state of nature and enter into a civil society, and "no rational Creature can be supposed to change his condition with an intention to be worse" (*Second Treatise*, sec. 131). Therefore, Locke's liberalism, by limiting the extent to which individuals can consent, also limits them in what they can consent to have the majority obligate them. For example, individuals cannot consent to absolute government:

For a man, not having the Power of his own Life, *cannot*, by Compact, or his own Consent, *enslave himself* to any one, nor put himself under the Absolute, Arbitrary Power of another, to take away his Life, when he pleases. No body can give more Power than he himself has; and he who cannot take away his own Life, cannot give another power over it. (*Second Treatise*, sec. 23–emphasis in the original)

Also, since in a state of nature individuals lack "arbitrary power over the life, liberty, or possession of another," neither can individuals consent to a political society with absolute power over some part of it. Thus, slavery, under anything but the most unusual condition, is abhorrent to a truly Lockean civil society (*Second Treatise*, secs. 17, 23, 24). Rather than condone the enslavement of self or others, the law of nature commands individuals to preserve themselves and the rest of personkind. To do so, nature bestows upon all individuals the previously discussed powers of judging and punishing. It is only these powers of preservation that individuals by consent can transfer to the political society (*Second Treatise*, sec. 135).

Thus, the same law of nature that prevents absolute liberty or license also prevents absolute majority control. It directs the majority to the same purpose that individuals pursue throughout their lives, that is, their self-preservation and the enjoyment of their liberty. Indeed, Locke states that the majority "can have no more than this. [Its] power . . . is *limited to the public good* of the society. It is a power, that hath no end but preservation. . . ." (Locke 1690, sec. 135–emphasis in the original). And for Locke, the public good is served only when the majority preserves the lives, liberty, and estates of all members of the community from the three principal defects of a state of nature: the absence of known and settled law, indifferent judges, and the power to back up punishment (*Second Treatise*, sec. 131). Thus, in a Lockean-styled civil society, the majority never becomes the supreme or absolute authority over individuals. Every rational individual's desire for self-preservation remains that.

Accordingly, Locke's liberalism further limits the majority by requiring the legislative and executive powers to be separated. This condition is imposed to ensure that the legislature responsible for formulating the community's law does not:

> exempt themselves from Obedience to the Laws they make, and suit the Law, both in its making and execution, to their own private advantage, and thereby come to a distinct interest from the rest of the Community, contrary to the end of Society and Government. (*Second Treatise*, sec. 143)

But Locke also recognizes that in separating the legislative and executive powers, the executor of the laws, like the legislature, must implement those laws in accordance with the public good of securing the life, liberty, and estates of the individual members of the civil society. Thus, by separating the legislative and executive powers, Locke creates a reciprocal relationship. For the same reasons the two functions are originally separated to guard against legislative excesses; once divided, the legislature has the obligation to protect the public good by reclaiming the executive power "when [it] finds cause, and to punish for any mall-administration against the laws" (*Second Treatise*, sec. 153).

In separating the legislative and executive powers, Locke's liberalism also teaches that to secure the public good and to protect the civil community from its government, the law of nature requires that the legislature, as the supreme power in the community, have specific limits placed upon its power (*Second Treatise*, secs. 134-142). To guarantee that the legislature can never easily exercise absolute and arbitrary control over the civil community, it is first obliged to rule through known and established laws applied equally to all within the community. Absent this condition, the individuals within the civil society would be no better off than if they remained in a state of nature (*Second Treatise*, secs. 137, 142). Second, the legislature must not delegate or transfer the power conferred upon it by the community to any other. By reason, "the power of the *Legislative* being derived from the People by a voluntary positive Grant . . . can be no other, than what that positive Grant conveyed, which being only to make *Laws*, and not to make *Legislators*" (*Second Treatise*, sec. 141).

Third, according to Locke's liberalism, the legislature cannot take from members of the community their property without their consent. Locke argues that lacking this limit on the legislature, individuals would truly have no claim to any property. He writes: "For I have truly no *Property* in that which another can . . . take from me, when he pleases, against my consent" (*Second Treatise*, sec. 138—emphasis in the original). Since an original purpose of government is the protection of property, "it is a mistake to think, that the . . . *Legislative Power* . . . can do what it will, and dispose of the Estates of the Subject *arbitrarily*, or take any part of them at pleasure" (*Second Treatise*, sec. 138). Thus, Locke concludes that the legislature cannot raise taxes on "the Property of the People, *without the Consent of the People*, given by themselves, or their Deputies" (*Second Treatise*, sec. 142).

To further discourage government from acting contrary to the trust bestowed upon it, Locke's liberalism retains the ultimate authority in a civil society to the individuals constituting it. In so doing, it recognizes that "every individual retains the . . . right to resist perceived threats to his property and existence, no matter what the source of those threats," whether the source is other individuals, the majority, or the government empowered to act for the majority (Pangle 1988, 255; *Second Treatise*, sec. 168). Though this right to resist is acknowledged, Locke remains pessimistic about the ability of a single or a few individuals to resist threats to their liberty. He notes that it is impossible for a few oppressed individuals to *"disturb the Government*, where the Body of the People do not think themselves concerned in it. . . ."" (*Second Treatise*, sec. 208—emphasis in the original). Yet it would appear to be in keeping with Locke's teaching to argue that the law of nature's obligation to preserve personkind when their own is not at risk requires those members of the community unaffected by the perceived threat to assist those whose liberty is so threatened.

Much like the individual within a political society, the community itself may perceive that the government created by consent to make the community one body has become dangerous to the society's continued preservation. And like the individual, the collective community also has the right to resist any attempt by government to make itself master over the community (*Second Treatise*, sec. 221). The civil society never forfeits or loses to the government it created the "native and Original Right it has to preserve itself" (*Second Treatise*, sec. 220). This right to preserve itself extends even to the civil society dissolving the existing government and instituting a new one (*Second Treatise*, secs. 218-223).

Though Locke's liberalism recognizes that an individual within a political society retains the right to resist perceived threats to his or her liberty, Locke writes that this right should and will be used infrequently. *"Great mistakes* in the ruling part, many wrong and inconvenient Laws and all the *slips* of humane frailty [should be] *born by the People, without mutiny or murmur"* (*Second Treatise*, sec. 225–emphasis in the original). Resistance, particularly that aimed at dissolving the existing government, should be reserved for when government has recorded "a long train of Abuses, Prevarications, and Artifices, all tending the same way" (*Second Treatise*, sec. 225).

By separating powers, setting limits on legitimate government power, and specifying remedies against government abuses, Locke defines a second face for liberty in a civil society. As noted earlier, the first face of liberty in a civil society is to "have a standing Rule to live by, common to every one of that Society, and made by the Legislative Power erected in it" (*Second Treatise*, sec. 22). In this context, liberty is security from those individuals who covet someone else's life, liberty, or estates. The power entrusted in the legislature, then, is to provide this security through known and equally applied laws.

The second face of civil liberty is a corollary to the first. If freedom in a civil society is defined, in part, as safety from those individuals who covet someone else's life, liberty, and property, freedom also must be defined as security against government doing the very things it was established to protect against. In short, liberty in a civil society must also include free-dom from government invasion of one's life, liberty, or estate. As Locke clearly articulates, this second face of civil liberty is accomplished best through imposing specific limits on government and providing the civil society the right to dissolve a government that invades the lives, liberty, and estates of its members.

Through these limits, this second face of civil liberty defines the relationship between government and members of the civil society. As Locke's limits on legislative power show, most of the liberty individuals enjoy from government is cast in negative terms limiting the actions that government can take. Phrased in this manner, the second face of civil liberty is an expression of negative freedom. "Negative freedom implies that people are free to the extent that government does not restrict preexisting ('natural')" rights (Glenn 1989, 188 fn. 2). It dictates that gov-ernment may not prohibit or place obstacles in the way of individuals freely exercising their liberty.

Negative freedom, though, does not require government to assist individuals who lack the economic, intellectual, or physical capacity to fully exercise their liberty (Goldstein 1981, 335). From this perspective, "mere incapacity" in being able to exercise a right (Berlin 1969, 122) or the government's unwillingness or failure to provide individuals "the means to enjoy freedom which they do not otherwise have" (Glenn 1989, 188 fn. 2) is not a lack of liberty (Berlin 1969, 122). Locke specifically recognizes this characteristic of his liberalism when he writes:

> . . . What if he neglects the care of his health, or his estate . . . ? Will the magistrate provide an express law, that such an one shall not become poor or sick? Laws provide, as much as possible, that the good health of subjects be not injured by the fraud or violence of others; they do not guard them from the negligence or ill husbandry of the possessors themselves. No man can be forced to be rich or healthful, whether he will or no. Nay, God himself will not save men against their will. (*A Letter concerning Toleration*, 23)

Taken as a whole, then, Lockean liberty is negative, and its government is minimalist. Government's sole obligation is the mutual protection of the members of the civil society that constituted it so that they may better enjoy the liberty unsecured in a state of nature. Government does this by establishing known and settled laws applied impartially toward all members of the community. Thus, the only thing that individuals within a civil society can expect from government is for it to secure their liberty. They cannot expect government to "ensure the distribution of civil goods so that each is to receive a comfortable level of existence" (Parry 1978, 112).

DISTINGUISHING BETWEEN THE PUBLIC AND PRIVATE SPHERES OF HUMAN LIFE

The negative freedom and minimalist government of Locke's liberalism are a response to an as yet unasked but compelling question: In what areas should persons be free to do or be what they are able to be, without interference from other persons or government (Berlin 1969, 122)? As captured in the limited purpose and power of civil government, a Lockean response is that persons are to remain free of outside interference in their lives from either other individuals or government in all areas that neither potentially or actually threaten their self-preservation, nor harm the lives, liberty, or estates of others. Areas of individual actions that do threaten self-preservation or harm the liberty of other persons reside in the public sphere of human existence. These areas are the proper and correct realm of government regulation and control in that they are likely to damage civil order and civil interests (Parry 1978, 84).

But areas of individual actions absent these qualities reside in the private sphere of human existence. Like the labor of their bodies and the work of their hands, these are a part of the property that all individuals have in their own persons to which "no Body has any Right to" but themselves (*Second Treatise*, sec. 27). As long as they remain private, they are beyond the regulation and control of government and entitled to its security.

In his writings, Locke clearly recognizes and accepts this principle that "some areas of human life are by right beyond the scope of government's coercive power"; that the coercive power of government "may surround and protect but may not penetrate" the liberty of those in whose name it governs (Glenn 1989, 61). Take, for instance, Locke's positions on government regulation of property and religion. Regarding the former, Locke writes that government "may have the power to make Laws for the regulating of *Property* between the Subjects one amongst the other" (*Second Treatise*, sec. 139). This power to regulate presumably exists because of the uses and acquisition of property. Possessing private property is clearly a natural right. But how it is acquired, such as through an exchange between individuals of money for real estate, or how it is used are likely to be infused with a public character. The public character of its acquisition and use makes otherwise private property subject to government regulation in order to prevent it from being used in ways harmful to one's self or others.

Regarding its role in religious affairs, Locke states directly and definitively that the jurisdiction of government "neither can nor ought in any manner be extended to the salvation of souls." This limitation exists because surrendering their salvation to another individual is something to which people cannot consent. "No man can so far abandon the care of his own salvation as blindly to leave it to the choice of another, as to compel any one to his religion." Thus, "the care of each man's soul . . . is left entirely to every man's self." It cannot be compelled by the "outward force" of government, but only through the private "inward and full persuasion" of an individual's mind (*A Letter concerning Toleration*, 10, 43-44). Applying this observation more generally, Locke appears to be saying that it is not the proper function of government to "institute truth" for those it governs (Parry 1978, 85).

Finding truth always remains with the individual. It is an essential means for securing their self-preservation. And as Locke teaches, all individuals possess "an absolute right to . . . self preservation, including the right to determine the means to it" (Glenn 1979, 1064). Therefore, in all aspects of a person's life that do not jeopardize this right or bring harm to another's life, liberty, or estate, the Lockean individual must be viewed as an autonomous moral agent (Kuflik 1984, 272; Parry 1978, 86), belonging to "himself and not to others or society as a whole" (*Bowers* v. *Hardwick*, 106 S. Ct. 2841 at 2851–Justice Blackmun dissenting). As such, people are at liberty in the private sphere of their life to engage in whatever truth, passions, and pleasures they deem desirable for their self-preservation. As an autonomous moral agent, a person possesses the freedom "to shape the most fundamental aspects of his or her life according to the dictates of his or her informed and conscientious judgment" (Perry 1988, 173). Thus, at the "heart of [Lockean] liberty is the right to define one's own concept of existence, of meaning, of the Universe, and of the mystery of human life. Beliefs about these matters [and others] could not define the attributes of personhood were they formed under compulsion of the state" (*Planned Parenthood of Southeastern Pennsylvania* v. *Casey*. 120 L. Ed. 2d 674 at 698).

But being autonomous moral agents does not free individuals to do whatever they happen to want to do (Kuflik 1984, 272). Instead, this obligates individuals to know reason. For Locke, reason is "the distinctive human faculty for self-preservation" (Tarcov 1984, 72). It is also the "Voice of God" within individuals directing them toward those actions that promote their self-preservation and away from their self-destruction (*First Treatise*, sec. 86). Through reason, individuals come to know and appreciate the limits imposed upon their liberty by the law of nature (*Second Treatise*, sec. 63). Knowing these limits, in turn, promotes self-preservation, thereby enabling individuals to better enjoy liberty. "For *Law* in its true Notion, is not so much the Limitation as *the direction of a free and intelligent Agent* to his proper Interest, and prescribes no farther than is for the general Good of those under the Law" (*Second Treatise*, sec. 57–emphasis in the original).

Thus, individuals are autonomous moral agents when they possess and are capable of applying the Lockean notion of reason to direct their private lives. This requires them to "take a critically reflective attitude toward [their lives] and the principles on which [they are] based." They "must be able to survey alternatives, reach decisions, and make a sincere effort to act as [they] decide [they] ought to act" (Kuflik 1984, 275). But in applying reason, Locke recognizes that all individuals will not reach the same conclusion as to what is moral. Some will clearly make choices that others would conclude are immoral. He notes that individuals are "apt to be misled by their passions, lusts, and other men" in the moral choices that they make in the private sphere of their lives (*A third Letter for Toleration*, 178). It is this failure to reach what others presume to be "correct" moral choices that one commentator, echoing Lockean sentiments, calls the "prize and price" of liberty:

> The prize of individual liberty is that some individuals will develop their moral capacities . . . including their capacity for wisdom, care, and their

responsibility for their own and others' welfare. . . . The price of . . . liberty is that some individuals will not develop their moral capacity. (Dunn 1990, 87)

Despite the "price" of liberty, Locke still teaches that within the private sphere government should not impose moral choices on individuals. Locke understands that coercing correct moral behavior in the private sphere does not, nor can it, make moral individuals. Morality is based on faith and belief rather than on force or coercion. Specifically addressing religious toleration, but also applicable to the more general concept of private morality, Locke writes:

All the life and power of true religion consists in the inward and full persuasion of the mind; and faith is not faith without believing. . . . And such is the nature of understanding, that it cannot be compelled to the belief of anything by outward force. Confiscation of estate, imprisonment, torment, nothing of that nature can have any such efficacy as to make men change the inward judgment that they have framed of things. (*A Letter concerning Toleration*, 10-11)

When faced with such coercive action against private morality, Locke's liberalism further recognizes that individuals are not "obliged by that law, against [their] conscience" (*A Letter concerning Toleration*, 43). In rejecting laws that violate their private morality, Locke's liberalism recognizes that individuals are asserting that:

there is . . . a sphere within which . . . individual[s] may assert the supremacy of [their] own will and rightfully dispute the authority of any human government—especially of any free government existing under a written constitution, to interfere with the exercise of that will. (*Roe* v. *Wade* 93 S. Ct. 756-759–Justice Douglass concurring and quoting *Jacobson* v. *Massachusetts* 197 U.S. 11 at 29)

Based upon the above reasoning, Locke's liberalism can be understood as stipulating that, in its dealing with the private sphere, government "should be modest . . . , and not too intent on enforcing virtue" (Feldman 1990, 137). It should not seek to impose the moral values of some groups in the political community, even the majority's values, onto dissenting groups. "The mere knowledge that other individuals do not adhere to one's value system cannot be a legally cognizable interest, let alone an interest that can justify invading the houses, hearts, and minds of citizens who choose to live their lives differently" (*Bowers* v. *Hardwick*, 106 S. Ct. 2841 at 2855-2856–Justice Blackmun dissenting). Thus, a government whose understanding of individual liberty is based upon the principles of Locke's liberalism does not try by force or coercion to transform individuals. Rather, it protects them (Farber and Sherry 1990, 13).

In reaching this conclusion, it is important to reiterate that Locke's liberalism protects moral choices that remain private only. Private moral choices that disrupt civil order or the civil interest of those individuals for which the political society was constituted lose their cloak of privacy. They enter the public sphere and are subject to government regulation and control. For example, religious practices that threaten to disrupt civil order are subject to public control (Parry 1978, 84). Locke writes that government cannot permit moral choices "contrary to . . . those moral rules which are necessary to the preservation of civil society" (*A Letter concerning Toleration*, 45).

For this same reason, certain public displays of other private moral choices also fall within the regulation and control of the civil society. For example, in the private sphere, individuals are free to indulge in unlimited sexual desire (Glenn 1989, 25). Yet the public exhibition of these sexual desires can be prohibited without offending individual liberty. Dissenting in *Bowers* v. *Hardwick* (106 S. Ct. 2841 at 2855-2856), Justice Blackmun captured this Lockean-inspired distinction between private moral choices and their public display:

> Statutes banning public sexual activities are entirely consistent with protecting the individual's liberty interest in decisions concerning sexual relations: the same recognition that those decisions are intensely private which justifies protecting them from government interference can justify protecting individuals from unwilling exposure to the sexual activities of others.

Government clearly is empowered to control and regulate public expressions of private moral choices disrupting the civil order and interests. In all other areas, individuals remain autonomous moral agents. But even here, government is not completely forbidden from acting. It is restricted *only* from using its coercive power to impose private moral behavior on individuals who would otherwise choose to behave or believe differently. Government remains free to take moral positions and to persuade individuals to make the moral choices that it deems best. Even in areas residing in the private sphere, Locke's liberalism recognizes that individuals cannot be completely free from attempted influence by others regarding the moral choices they make. What matters is the form that this influence takes. It is "one thing to persuade, another to command; one thing to press with arguments, another with penalties" (*A Letter concerning Toleration*, 11).

Serving as the one body and voice of the civil society, government possesses the same power as the individuals within it to persuade persons in regard to the private moral choices they make. Like individual members of the civil society, government, too, "has commission to admonish, exhort, convince another of error, and by reason draw him into truth" (*A Letter concerning Toleration*, 11). In short, Locke's liberalism does not require or expect government to be morally indifferent, only that it communicates its morality through persuasion based upon reason and not the coercive power of law. Locke's liberalism admonishes government to accept that "all normal adults have the capacity for responsible moral behavior" and to pursue *"individually chosen* right conduct, or moral goodness" rather than coerced moral behavior (Dunn 1990, 86, 91–emphasis in the original).

3

Locke's Liberalism and the Constitution

To reiterate an important point in Chapter 1: any middle position on abortion capable of demonstrating how government must be both pro-choice and anti-abortion, thus also setting the outer limits of abortion policy, must itself be firmly grounded in this nation's constitutional heritage and the philosophical ideas shaping it. This precondition means that any successful middle position on abortion must be cognitive of the nexus between John Locke's liberalism presented in Chapter 2 and the political thinking of the founding generation and the framers of the Constitution.

The traditional perspective on America's political and constitutional founding once exalted John Locke and his liberal theory of individual rights as the dominant influence on the political thinking of the founding generation (i.e., Hartz 1955). "From this perspective John Locke's *Two Treatises of Government* looked like 'the textbook of the American Revolution'" (Dworetz 1990, 6). But through more than twenty years of revisionist historiography that began in the late 1960s, the teachings of John Locke were denigrated until they achieved near untouchable status. In place of Locke, a new generation of scholars sought to advance republican civic virtue as the principal philosophical outlook of American independence and constitutionalism (e. g. Bailyn 1967; Wills 1979).

But today, neo-traditionalists on America's political and constitutional founding are returning Locke to his rightful place among the political philosophers whose writings and teachings informed and influenced the political thinking of eighteenth century America and the constitution it would ultimately produce (i.e., Dworetz 1990; Lutz 1988, 11; Jaffa 1946,

76-109; Macedo 1987, 128-129; McDonald 1985; Pangle 1988; Richards 1989). For the more zealous redeemers of Locke,

> in relation to the most crucial issues of the Anglo-American dispute (for instance, representation, taxation, consent, religious liberty, the limits of civil authority per se, the right and duty of revolution, and the ultimate sovereignty of the people) . . . the historical-textual evidence testifies consistently and often explicitly in the language of "Locke on Government." (Dworetz 1990, 8)

They conclude, therefore, that the founding generation can easily be considered "the thoughtful posterity" of the seventeenth century English philosopher (Richards 1989, 26).

Less strident voices among the neo-traditionalists also reaffirm Locke. But they do so in a more realistic appraisal of his influence in relation to other philosophers. Locke, they conclude, "was undeniably important [to the founding generation], but there is no single author, let alone a single text, that can account for . . . the core of American constitutionalism" (Luntz 1988, 11). Thomas Pangle's *The Spirit of Modern Republicanism* (1988) is typical of this more modest, yet still significant, claim of Lockean influence on eighteenth century American political thinking. He writes:

> It is not unreasonable to contend that Locke's influence on the eighteenth century, especially in America, was massive; but those caught up in the spiritual revolution he did so much to inspire . . . probably did not always grasp the full meaning or momentum of the new theoretical current he helped to set in motion. . . . It would seem that the most theoretical minded of the Framers followed Locke in at least the following decisive way. They tried to find the surest ground of human security and dignity in a natural, competitive self-assertion: in an individualism that is properly regulated, not so much by deference to tradition and custom . . . as by *reason* dominating passion and sentiment through *law* that expresses indirect—but radical—popular sovereignty. (Pangle 1988, 126-127—emphasis in the original)

As Pangle's comments suggest, these moderate neo-traditionalists claim neither that the founding generation and the framers understood nor that they applied Locke's liberalism perfectly or consistently. The expression of a Lockean-styled notion of equality in the Declaration of Independence but their apparent abandonment of this principle in the Constitution's original toleration and acceptance of slavery is a good case in point (McDonald 1985, 50-55).

For the purpose of presenting a Lockean perspective on abortion, these more modest reassessments of the nexus between Locke's liberalism and the political thinking of the founding generation are sufficient in their own right to justify applying Locke to this contemporary policy debate. For it is not necessary to show that Locke was the sole or even the most significant influence on the political thinking of eighteenth century America. Indeed, no responsible scholar would ever claim that the Constitution and the political thinking informing it was purely Lockean (Jaffa 1984, 106). Nor is it necessary to show that when the founding generation and the framers did rely on Locke they were always consistent in their application of Lockean principles. A less definitive conclusion on both points of contention is sufficient. It is only necessary to establish that Locke was one of the significant influences on the founding generation and the framers of the Constitution, particularly in regard to individual liberty and to know in what ways their thinking was Lockean-inspired or -styled.

LOCKE, THE FOUNDING GENERATION, AND THE FRAMERS

For proof that before the establishment of civil society personkind resides in a state of nature, Locke directed his readers' attention in *The Second Treatise on Government*, to America. He wrote: "In the beginning all the World was *America*" (sec. 49–emphasis in the original). Locke's observations on America were particularly evidenced in his discussion on property. For example, Locke noted:

> The greatest part of *things really useful* to the Life of Man . . . such as the necessity of subsisting made the first Commoners of the World look after, as it doth the *Americans* now, are generally things of *short duration*; such as, if they are not consumed by use, will decay and perish of themselves. (*Second Treatise*, sec. 46–emphasis in the original)

Locke's reference to America suggests that he saw the New World as empirical evidence supporting the correctness of his philosophical thinking. But Locke's reliance on America for this proof also suggests that "for all [its] resonance with Locke's ideas, many of the principles and assumptions of American constitutionalism were operative [in the 1600s] before Locke published his *Second Treatise on Government*" (Lutz 1988, 10-11). For example, before Locke's theory of civil society, the American colonists were already organizing and governing themselves through consensual compacts (Feldman 1990, 173-174). Take, for instance, the Pilgrims who first formed a religious compact organizing themselves as a church and who next formed a business compact to finance their migration to America. Upon reaching America, they formed yet another compact to provide for their self-government. In the Mayflower Compact, they consented "to combine ourselves into a civil body politick" providing for self-government (Feldman 1990, 173). Thus based upon this and other examples, some scholars, while still recognizing Locke's influence on the founding generation and the framers of the Constitution, suggest that, at least initially, "it makes more sense to call Locke an American than it does to call [17th century] America Lockean" (Lutz 1988, 11).

To say at the time of the *Second Treatise* that Locke was more American than America was Lockean does not undermine the relevance of his political writings and teachings to the founding generation and the framers of the Constitution. To the contrary, acknowledging Locke's appreciation of seventeenth century American colonial experience only serves to bring the two closer together. Recognizing the early connection between Locke's liberalism and America makes it easier to understand why by the time of the revolution "most Americans had absorbed Locke's work as a kind of political gospel" (Dworetz 1990, 15–quoting Carl Becker). It was a political theory of liberty and government informed, at least in part, by their own experience.

The widespread acceptance in America of Locke's liberalism occurred principally through what might be called "socialization from the pulpit." In their sermons, the clergy in America, particularly in New England, taught their congregations not only about God and religion but also political theory. This teaching was heavily influenced by Locke's liberalism. As one recent commentator explains:

> The clergy were demonstrably conversant in Locke's writings, and they had similar "religious preoccupations." They openly embraced Locke's political ideas—for example, the justification for revolution . . . *and* they shared the general philosophical perspective within which those ideas took shape. Moreover, the ministers conveyed the Lockean message, regularly and with great moral authority, to their congregations, by whom they were taken very seriously indeed. (Dworetz 1990, 32)

The ability of the clergy to have such a profound influence on their congregations was enhanced by the colonial experience already noted to have influenced at least some of Locke's political thinking. In effect, the members of the clergy were presenting to their congregations a political theory that by no small accident coincided with and was partially influenced by their own experience. In this regard, then, Locke's liberalism was "instinctive to the American mind" and appealed to the colonists' common sense (Hartz 1955, 62). Since Lockean-styled thought was so in tune with the colonial experience, it is easy to see how this line of thinking influenced both the founding generation's thinking about independence and the framers' thinking about constitutions. These Lockean thoughts were simply in accord with the goals of both (McDonald 1985, 66).

THE FOUNDING GENERATION AND FRAMERS' USE OF LOCKEAN-STYLED LIBERALISM

The instinctive and common sense appeal of Locke's liberalism to the founding generation was given great expression through the overwhelming success of Thomas Paine's *Common Sense*. This pamphlet was an immediate success, selling an estimated 150,000 copies. Through the overwhelming popularity of *Common Sense*, Paine converted "countless men and women to the cause of independence" (Foner 1984, 10). Paine promoted this conversion to independence with ideas that had their own intellectual roots in Lockean-styled liberalism (Kramnick 1985, 38). For example, Paine shared with Locke an understanding that civil or political societies are formed primarily to better secure liberty that individuals are unable to secure for themselves:

> Thus necessity, like a gravitating power, would soon form our newly arrived emigrants into society, the reciprocal blessings of which, would supersede, and render the obligations of law and government unnecessary while they remained perfectly just to one another; but as nothing but heaven is impregnable to vice, it will unavoidable happen, that in proportion as they surmount the first difficulties of emigration . . . they will relax in their duty and attachment to each other; and this remissness, will point out the necessity, of establishing some form of government to supply the defects of moral virtue. . . . Here then is the origin and rise of government, namely, a mode rendered necessary by the inability of moral virtue to govern the world; here to is the design and end of government, viz. freedom and security. (*Common Sense*, 66)

Like Locke, Paine also spoke of religious tolerance, implying that religious diversity would more likely produce correct moral behavior than if everyone was of the same faith:

> As to religion, I hold it to be the indispensable duty of all government, to protect all conscientious professors thereof, and I know of no other business which government hath to do therewith. . . . I fully and conscientiously believe, that it is the will of the Almighty, that there should be diversity of religious opinions among us: It affords a larger field for our christian kindness. Were we all of one way of thinking, our religious dispositions would want matter for probation. (*Common Sense*, 108-109)

Beyond Paine, the Declaration of Independence was perhaps the clearest expression of Locke or Lockean-styled thought (Jaffa 1984). In the second sentence, Thomas Jefferson states:

> We hold these truths to be self-evident, that all men are created equal, that they are endowed by their Creator with certain unalienable Rights, that among these are Life, Liberty, and the pursuit of Happiness. That to secure these rights, Governments are instituted among Men, deriving their just powers from the consent of the governed. That whenever any form of Government becomes destructive of these ends, it is the Right of the People to alter or to abolish it, and to institute a new Government. . . .

Through these powerful and majestic words, Jefferson echoed many of the major assumptions and principles of Lockean-styled liberalism: individuals possess natural rights; individuals form government to better secure these rights; arising from consent, government authority is by nature limited; and individuals can dissolve or rebel against government that does not secure their liberty or that violates it (Diamond 1976, 15-19; Richards 1989, 80-81). In fact, Lockean-styled liberalism was so expressive in the Declaration, passages within it read *as if* a copy of Locke's *Second Treatise* laid open before Jefferson as he was writing them. For example, David Richards in his book *Foundations of American Constitutionalism*, (1989, 80-81) notes the markedly strong similarity between Jefferson's justification in the Declaration for the American Revolution and Locke's justification in the *Second Treatise* for dissolving government. (See also Jaffa 1984, 104-108).

In the immediate post-independence period, Lockean-styled liberalism continued to influence political thinking in America. This sustained reliance was most readily apparent during the drafting and ratification of the Constitution in which Lockean-styled liberalism served as a philosophical bridge linking the Declaration of Independence and the Constitution. Though it is now commonplace to examine the Constitution in isolation from the Declaration of Independence, the latter with its powerful articulation of Lockean-styled liberalism was the theory of individual rights guiding the delegates at the Constitutional Convention (Henkin 1991, 84). Indeed, "those who framed the United States Constitution were committed to the idea of rights as expressed in the Declaration of Independence" (Henkin 1990, 112).

For example, as Jefferson did when he wrote the Declaration, the framers in the preamble of the Constitution accepted the Lockean-styled notion of consent. It is here that they also announced, in clear Lockean-styled prose, that the purpose of the Constitution was to *"secure the blessing of liberty to ourselves and our posterity"* (emphasis added). The preamble, then, inseparably joined the Constitution to the Declaration of Independence, though this fact is largely ignored in contemporary constitutional analysis. By shaping the preamble as they did, the framers clearly understood that the Declaration of Independence was principally a statement on the legitimate ends of government, and that those ends reflected the Lockean purpose of securing liberty. The Constitution, on the other hand, was intended to be the means by which these ends of legitimate government were to be achieved (Diamond 1976, 318; Himmelfarb 1990, 174). In this regard, framers such as James Madison saw the Declaration as being fundamental to the proper understanding of the Constitution (Himmelfarb 1990, 170).

From this brief discussion of the link between the Declaration of Independence and the Constitution, "it would hardly be an exaggeration to say that the most fundamental pronouncements made in connection with the framing and the ratification of the Constitution [were] restatements of the principles articulated in the second sentence of the Declaration" (Himmelfarb 1990, 170-171). Just as the principles in the Declaration were Lockean-influenced, so, too, were the debates between the Federalists and Anti-Federalists surrounding both the framing and ratification of the Constitution. This influence is so clearly apparent that the Constitutional Convention and the ratification debates can be understood, in part, as a practical effort at constructing a government around the Lockean-styled liberalism expressed in the Declaration of Independence, including Locke's discussion on the dissolution of government. The final outcome of both the Convention and the ratification process was the dissolution of one government unable to secure liberty and the creation of another better able to do so.

For example, in proposing to dissolve the government established under the Articles of Confederation, the framers exhibited a Lockean understanding of why government comes into existence and its purpose once constituted. Government, they recognized, is formed because the "passions of men will not conform to the dictates of reason" (Hamilton, *Federalist Papers 15*, 110). Government comes into being because it is needed to protect individuals against those who will not live by reason. Thus, the framers understood that government was necessary to guarantee individuals their natural right of self-preservation. They understood that this "great principle" declared that the "safety and happiness of society are the objects at which all political institutions are aimed and to which all such institutions must be sacrificed" (Madison, *Federalist Papers 43*, 279).

By recognizing the need and purpose of government, both the Federalist supporters and Anti-Federalist opponents of the Constitution equally accepted the Lockean principle that legitimate government was based on consent only. Both sides in the ratification debate accepted that "all [government] power is naturally invested in, and consequently derived from, the people; that magistrates therefore are their *trustees* and *agents*, at all times amenable to them" (*Proposed Amendments by the Virginia Convention*, 219). Or, as James Madison so eloquently and succinctly phrased it, "The people are the only legitimate fountain of power" (*Federalist Papers 49*, 313).

By acknowledging that legitimate government must be based upon consent, the Federalists and the Anti-Federalists also accepted, as did Locke, that individuals cannot consent to absolute government,

> that there are certain natural rights, of which men, when they form a social compact, cannot deprive or divest their posterity: among which are the enjoyment of life and liberty, with the means of acquiring, possessing, and protecting property, and pursuing and obtaining happiness and safety. (*Proposed Amendments by the Virginia Convention*, 1788)

Therefore, both sides in the debate over the proposed Constitution accepted the Lockean principle of limited government. They agreed that government is "properly directed to the pursuit of limited ends, namely the security of individual rights; and there was very little debate about limited government in this fundamental sense" (Storing 1981, 53). For instance, their debate over the necessity of a bill of rights was mainly "an extension of the general debate over the nature of limited government" (Storing 1981, 67). In this debate, both sides claimed the greater allegiance to this Lockean principle.

For example, the Anti-Federalists claimed that to truly limit the new national government, the proposed Constitution needed a bill of rights. George Mason clearly expressed this concern to his fellow delegates at the Constitutional Convention when he explained why he opposed the final draft of the Constitution. According to Mason, the government proposed by the new Constitution was not limited enough because there was "no declaration of any kind, for preserving the liberty of the press, or the trial by jury in civil causes; nor against the danger of standing armies in time of peace" (Ketchum 1986, 173-175). In rebuttal to Mason and other Anti-Federalist critics of the proposed constitution, Federalists argued that any need for a bill of rights was preempted by the limited nature of the powers assigned to the new central government (Macedo 1987, 32). For example, Hamilton argued: "In strictest sense, the people surrender nothing; and as they retain everything they have no need of particular reservations" (*Federalist Papers 84*, 513).

The political thinking of both the Federalists and Anti-Federalists also exhibited a Lockean-styled distinction between the public and private sphere of human life. Writing specifically about Federalist thinking but generally applicable also to the Anti-Federalists, Thomas Pangle observes that their understanding of

> liberty [was] twofold: it comprise[d] both political rights and "private" rights, both "public" and "personal" liberty. And the private or personal liberty include[d] not only security of person, property, opinion, and religious persuasion; it include[d] as well the liberty to remain in a private station, the right to refuse most of the burdens and responsibilities of republicanism. (Pangle 1988, 117)

This private liberty, in particular, was recognized to be "unalienable and personal rights of [all individuals] over which it is not necessary for a good government to have control" (*Dissent of the Pennsylvania Minority* 1787).

When the Federalists made this distinction between the public and private liberty, a principal way in which they sought to secure the sanctity of the latter was by protecting property rights (Mindle 1989, 577). Like that of Locke, the framers' understanding of property was quite broad: recognizing a property interest both in one's self and possessions. It included "the property which individuals have in their opinions, their religion, their passions, and their faculties" (Mindle 1989, 583–quoting Madison). Thus, property rights encompassed everything individuals could reasonably claim belonged exclusively to themselves and, therefore, were private (Mindle 1989, 583). And for Federalists, such as Madison, the protection of these property interests was "the first object of government" (*Federalist Paper 10*, 79).

While sharing their opponents' passion for property, the Anti-Federalists provided an additional distinction between the public and private sphere of human life in their concern for and desire to protect religious liberty. Though they argued that promoting morality, virtue, and religion was a proper responsibility for government (Kramnick 1987, 58), the Anti-Federalists also recognized that none of these things could be achieved through government coercion, and that how moral, virtuous, or religious a person was had to remain an individual choice. Addressing the private nature of religious liberty in particular, the Virginia Ratification Convention noted:

> The manner of discharging [religion] can be directed only by reason and conviction, not by force or violence; and therefore all men have an equal, natural, unalienable right to the free exercise of religion, according to the dictates of conscience, and . . . no particular religious sect or society ought to be favored or established, by law, in preference to others. (Ketcham 1986, 221)

Thus, it is possible to conclude that in drafting and ratifying the Constitution, both the Federalists and Anti-Federalists undertook to secure conditions favorable to the pursuit of happiness. They recognized the significance of man's spiritual nature, of his feeling and of his intellect. They knew that only a part of the pain, pleasure and satisfaction of life are to be found in material things. They sought to protect Americans in their beliefs, their thoughts, their emotions and sensations (*Bowers* v. *Hardwick* 106 S. Ct. 2841 at 2852–Justice Blackmun dissenting and quoting *Stanley* v. *Georgia* 394 U.S. 557 at 564).

LOCKEAN-STYLED LIBERALISM IN THE CONSTITUTION

Because the political thinking of the Federalists and Anti-Federalists was influenced, at least partially, by a Lockean-styled liberalism, it is not surprising that the original text of the Constitution and the first ten amendments, which were added to it by the First Congress in response to the ratification debates, exhibit the effects of that influence. The Lockean-styled nature of the Constitution is particularly evident in its strong emphasis on securing liberty through government while maintaining limits on its power over individuals. For example, beyond the preamble, the Constitution incorporates the Lockean principle of limited government into the document in such ways as dividing power into three functionally separate branches of government and enumerating legislative powers. In addition, the Constitution's requirement in Article I that "all Bills for raising Revenue shall originate in the House of Representatives" reflects the Lockean concern with protecting property. By entrusting the popularly elected chamber of the Congress with the power to initiate bills for raising revenue, the framers can be understood as securing the Lockean limit that the legislative branch "must *not raise Taxes* on the Property of the People, *without the Consent of the People*, given by themselves, or their Deputies" (*Second Treatise*, sec. 142).

The Lockean emphasis on limits is further presented in the Constitution's recognition of the private sphere of human existence. For example, the moral autonomy possessed by the Lockean individual is evident in the Constitution's promotion of religious toleration. Both Article VI's prohibition on a religious test for holding public office and the First Amendment's prohibition on the establishment or infringement of the free exercise of religion reflect this principle of Lockean-styled liberalism.

The Constitution further recognizes the Lockean distinction between the public and private sphere through the expansive nature of liberty protected by the Bill of Rights. As the Supreme Court observed in *West Virginia State Board of Education* v. *Barnette* (319 U.S. 624 at 638): "The very purpose of a Bill of Rights [is] to withdraw certain subjects from the vicissitudes of political controversy, to place them beyond the reach of majorities." Consider for example the often maligned and unfortunately rarely relied upon Ninth Amendment. It is perhaps the clearest constitutional recognition of the expansive nature of the liberty secured by the Bill of Rights. It is a constitutional acknowledgment that "there are fundamental personal rights . . . which are protected from abridgement by the Government though not specifically mentioned in the Constitution" (*Griswold* v. *Connecticut* 381 U.S. 479 at 492–Justice Goldberg concurring).

These "fundamental personal rights" include liberty closely associated with the private sphere and the moral autonomy that accompanies it—liberty that is "essential to the orderly pursuit of happiness by free men" (*Meyers* v. *Nebraska* 262 U.S. 390 at 399). Thus, as Justice Harlan wrote in dissent in *Poe* v. *Ullman* (367 U.S. 497), the liberty protected by the Constitution

> is not a series of isolated points pricked out in terms of the taking of property; the freedom of speech, press, and religion; . . . the freedom from unreasonable searches and seizures; and so on. It is a rational continuum which, broadly speaking, includes a freedom from all substantial arbitrary impositions and purposeless restraints. . . . (367 U.S. 497 at 543)

But with its Lockean-styled roots, the Constitution traditionally has been read and interpreted as limiting liberty as well as securing it. In this regard, the Constitution can be understood as incorporating a Lockean distinction between liberty and license:

> The liberty secured by the Constitution . . . to every person within its jurisdiction does not import an absolute right in each person to be, at all times and in all circumstances, wholly free from restraint . . . . (*Jacobson* v. *Massachusetts* 197 U.S. 11 at 26)

The liberty limiting nature of this distinction is clearly evident in many of the rights secured by the Bill of Rights. For example, both the Second and Third Amendments limit the liberty they protect. The Second Amendment secures "the right of the people to keep and bear arms." But this liberty is limited by its association with a "well-regulated militia being necessary to the security of a free State."

Similarly, the Third Amendment protects individuals in the privacy of their homes by forbidding the quartering of soldiers in private residences. But this privacy is conditional. It applies only to times of peace. In times of war, the Constitution allows this liberty interest in the privacy of an individual's home to be infringed. The limited nature of liberty extends even to such fundamental rights as the freedom of speech. As Justice Holmes wrote in *Schenck* v. *United States* (249 U.S. 47), "the most stringent protection of free speech would not protect a man in falsely shouting fire in a theatre, and causing a panic" (Curry et al. 1989, 445).

The conclusion to be drawn from this discussion, then, is that the idea of liberty in the Constitution "embodies a promise that a certain sphere of individual liberty will be kept largely beyond the reach of government" (*Thornburgh* v. *American College of Obstetricians and Gynecologists* 90 L. Ed. 2d 779 at 800). It is a promise that if not purely Lockean-inspired, is at least Lockean-styled. It presents an appreciation that the Constitution embodies a limiting and power-constraining logic (Barnett 1989, 17) that does not try to make a perfectly moral society as much as it tries to prevent a bad one from occurring (Feldman 1990, 137). Rather, it is a Lockean-styled recognition that attempts to invade the private sphere of human life "are excessive and often lead to monstrous immorality" (Goldwin 1986, 35). The most apparent "immorality" is the loss of liberty. But in equally Lockean manner, the Constitution recognizes that liberty, itself, must have some limits placed upon it if the individual is to be truly free.

4

A Lockean Understanding of the Liberty Interest in the Abortion Decision

As presented in Chapter 2, Lockean-styled liberalism requires government and the majority within the civil community to tolerate the private moral choices of others with which they disagree. For this reason, public policies dealing with areas of morality over which reasonable individuals are likely to disagree must be moderate. They must seek a compromise or some middle position that respects the diversity in moral opinions (Macedo 1990, 72).

Abortion policy is clearly such an area in which government must tolerate and incorporate diverging moral viewpoints. As Chapter 1 notes, reasonable people can and do disagree intensely over the morality of abortion. Faced with unwanted and unplanned pregnancies, many women, acting as autonomous moral agents, choose to terminate these pregnancies through abortion. But even though their choice may strike many in the civil community as immoral, Lockean-styled government is obligated to tolerate this private decision as far as toleration means government restraining itself from using its authority and power to prohibit or coerce women from choosing to resolve unwanted pregnancies through abortion. Writing for the Court's plurality in *Planned Parenthood of Southeastern Pennsylvania* v. *Casey* (120 L. Ed. 2d 674 at 697) Justices O'Connor, Souter, and Kennedy captured the core of this Lockean obligation:

> Men and women of good conscience can disagree, and we suppose some always shall disagree, about the profound moral and spiritual implications of terminating a pregnancy, even in its earliest stage. Some of us as individuals find abortion offensive to our most basic principles of morality, but that

cannot control our decision. *Our obligation is to define the liberty of all, not to mandate our own moral code*. (Emphasis added)

Though Lockean-styled liberalism demands official tolerance regarding private moral choices, as Chapter 2 also discusses, government need not remain morally indifferent or neutral to these choices. Just as individual members of the civil community do, government retains the ability through moral suasion to foster what it deems to be correct moral choices. In this regard, Lockean-styled liberalism recognizes that there is a basic difference between government interference with or prohibition of private moral choices and government encouragement of alternative choices. Lockean-styled liberalism prohibits the first but condones the latter.

This authority or power of government to promote what it deems as being morally correct extends to private moral choices surrounding an individual's sexual and procreative liberty, including abortion. Justice Stevens expressed this Lockean recognition when he wrote: "Society has every right to encourage its individual members to follow particular traditions in expressing affection for one another and in gratifying their personal desires" (*Bowers* v. *Hardwick* 106 S. Ct. 2841 at 2858–Justice Stevens dissenting).

Neither the traditional pro-life nor pro-choice perspectives articulate the Lockean obligation of moral tolerance without moral indifference. The pro-life position clearly is not indifferent to the morality of abortion. But it completely lacks moral tolerance. As noted in Chapter 1, the professed goal of pro-life advocates is to impose through the coercive power of government their anti-abortion morality on the whole of the civil community. In contrast, the standard pro-choice perspective embraces moral tolerance of abortion, and on this point it is closer to the Lockean perspective than the pro-life position is. But pro-choice advocates apply their appreciation of moral tolerance too rigidly in that they expect government to be completely indifferent to the morality of abortion. They reject the claim that government acts legitimately when it takes actions designed to promote what it believes to be correct moral reasoning on abortion by encouraging women to adopt this reasoning as they consider ways to resolve their unwanted pregnancies.

Thus, neither the pro-life nor pro-choice perspectives reflect a Lockean understanding of a woman's liberty interest in the abortion decision, particularly its prescription of moral tolerance without moral indifference. Therefore, the remainder of Chapter 4 elaborates more fully this Lockean understanding of a woman's liberty interest in the abortion decision and its balance between moral tolerance without moral indifference. First, a Lockean defense of the private nature of the abortion decision is made. Second, the liberty interest in the abortion decision as an exercise of negative freedom is examined through a discussion on public funding of abortion. Finally, how government can practice moral tolerance toward the abortion decision without moral indifference is examined.

ABORTION AS A PRIVATE, MORAL CHOICE

From a Lockean perspective, abortion can be understood as residing among the individual, personal, and private decisions that do not involve, and therefore lay beyond, the minimalist purposes for which government is originally established (Friedman 1983, 17). In particular, a woman's liberty interest in abortion is closely associated with her expectations of sexual and procreative liberty. As discussed in Chapter 2, the Lockean designation of individuals as autonomous moral agents means that in the private sphere of their existence, they are free to engage in any sexual intimacy they desire as long as that behavior neither threatens their own self-preservation nor brings harm to others. The importance of this sexual liberty is underscored by the further recognition that many individuals define themselves in "significant ways through their intimate sexual relationships with others." That so many individuals do so suggests that "there may be many 'right' ways of conducting those relationships, and that much of the richness of a relationship will come from the freedom an individual has to *choose* the form and nature of these intensely personal bonds" (*Bowers* v. *Hardwick* 106 S. Ct. 2841 at 2851-2852–Justice Blackmun dissenting).

To freely express their sexual liberty "to engage in heterosexual sex is a major reason why women, seek [the availability of] reliable birth control and abortion" (Petchesky 1990, 302). For these women, the exercise of their sexual liberty is closely associated with the liberty to make choices regarding procreation. Procreative liberty is defined as both "the freedom not to reproduce and the freedom to reproduce when, with whom, and by what means one chooses" (Robertson 1983, 406). Though procreative liberty concerns both dimensions of reproductive choice, popular and legal discussions of this liberty routinely emphasize the ability of individuals to express themselves through heterosexual sex without fear of unwanted pregnancies or parenthood. Conceptualized as such, procreative liberty is basically about freeing individuals to pursue heterosexual intimacy for pleasurable and recreational reasons, and not just for reproduction. This means if individuals are to enjoy the liberty to choose not to reproduce, they also must have the freedom to choose the methods by which to secure their ability to engage in nonreproductive sex, whether that be the freedom to prevent reproduction through the use of contraceptives or to terminate an unwanted pregnancy resulting from contraceptive failure or unprotected sexual intercourse.

From a Lockean perspective, that this procreative liberty is "one of the basic civil rights of [individuals]. . . . fundamental to the very existence and survival of the race" is by no means an overstatement (*Skinner* v. *Oklahoma* 316 U.S. 535 at 541). Decisions about procreation, both to reproduce or not, are among the most private and personal decisions that individuals are likely to have to make. The intensely personal nature of procreative decisions means that the primary responsibility for them must rest "squarely in the private sector of our society" and among autonomous moral agents "free from unwarranted governmental intrusion into matters so fundamentally affecting a person as the decision whether to bear or beget a child" (*Thornburgh* v. *American College of Obstetricians and Gynecologists* 90 L. Ed. 2d 779 at 806–Justice Stevens concurring). Indeed, to allow government to invade this liberty would cause "irreparable injury" to individuals with "no redemption" available to them (*Skinner* v. *Oklahoma* 316 U.S. 535 at 541).

Thus, any government invasion into private procreative decisions makes a mockery of both the Lockean distinction between the public and private sphere of human existence and the principle of limited government. Such invasion would make government's authority virtually limitless, with no aspect of an individual's life being meaningfully private. If it were possible to conclude that procreative decisions do not reside in the private sphere, then "we might almost as well not have any laws of constitutional limitation . . . because a constitutional law inadequate to deal with such an outrage would be too feeble, in method and doctrine, to deal with a very great amount of equally outrageous materials" (Black 1970, 32).

What is true about the general liberty interest in procreation is equally true about a woman's liberty interest in decisions about how best to resolve her unwanted pregnancy. The private sphere of human existence, with its guarantee of moral autonomy, is "broad enough to encompass a woman's decision whether or not to terminate her pregnancy" (*Roe* v. *Wade* 93 S. Ct. 705 at 727). It is clearly a decision that must be "exercised without public scrutiny and in defiance of the contrary opinion of the sovereign or other third parties" (*Bellotti* v. *Baird* 443 99 S. Ct. 3035 at 3054–Justice Stevens concurring; see also *Doe* v. *Bolton* 93 S. Ct. 739; *Planned Parenthood of Central Missouri* v. *Danforth* 96 S. Ct. 2831; *City of Akron* v. *Akron Center for Reproductive Health* 76 L. Ed. 2d 687; *Planned Parenthood of Kansas City Missouri* v. *Ashcroft* 76 L. Ed. 2d 733).

The private nature of the abortion decision stems in part from the intensely personal and private effects that pregnancy has on a woman. Pregnancy is an "irreducible physical burden" that requires the "renunciation of bodily health and well-being for many months, perhaps with permanent physical consequences" (Petchesky 1990, 379). A woman who "carries a child to full term is subject to anxieties, to physical constraints, to pain that only she must bear" (*Planned Parenthood of Southeastern Pennsylvania* v. *Casey* 120 L. Ed. 2d 674 at 698-699). Thus a woman's suffering during pregnancy is just "too personal and intimate" to allow government to force her choice about how to resolve an unwanted pregnancy (120 L. Ed. 2d 674 at 699).

To permit government to impose pregnancy on a woman who would otherwise choose to terminate it, would only intensify the suffering and other inconveniences associated with being pregnant. More important, if government was able to force a woman to carry her pregnancy to full term, this act would be the equivalent to involuntary servitude or enslavement, regardless of how temporary that bondage would be (Petchesky 1990, 379). It would, in effect, make government the master over the woman carrying the developing fetal-being. As discussed in Chapter 2, Lockean-styled liberalism does not allow for this kind of enslavement or involuntary servitude except for a few special and extreme circumstances (see *Second Treatise*, secs. 22-24).

When understood in this manner, for government to impose its anti-abortion morality on a woman experiencing an unwanted pregnancy would clearly violate her liberty to be free from external compulsion to shape the fundamental aspects of her life. In particular, coerced moral behavior on abortion would cause a woman to accept "substantial, prolonged sacrifices" in another's behalf. A woman forced into "giving her body and its resources to the development of another body, makes a sacrifice that takes its toll on her physical, emotional, and often financial, health, during pregnancy and afterward" (Dunn 1990, 110).

This same logic also prohibits government from relegating the final decision over abortion from the women experiencing unwanted pregnancies to their spouses or the biological "fathers" of the fetal-beings. Government cannot delegate power it does not possess anymore than it can delegate authority originally bestowed upon it through consent (*Second Treatise*, sec. 141). Since government generally lacks the authority to impose involuntary servitude on individuals who have not violated the community's laws, it can by no means grant this power to enslave to some for exercising over others. Thus, from a Lockean understanding of a woman's liberty interest in abortion, spousal consent laws are impermissible.

Spousal consent effectively gives another person (the husband or biological father) absolute control and veto over an intensely private moral choice. In so doing, spousal notification temporarily enslaves a woman experiencing an unwanted pregnancy to someone else and his concept of correct moral behavior. Justices O'Connor, Kennedy, and Souter, writing for the Court's plurality in *Planned Parenthood of Southeastern Pennsylvania* v. *Casey*, captured well the severity of this untenable domination encouraged through spousal consent laws:

> A husband has no enforceable right to require a wife to advise him before she exercises personal choices. If a husband's interest in the potential life of the [fetal-being] outweighs a wife's liberty, the State could require a married woman to notify her husband before she uses postfertilization contraceptives. Perhaps next in line would be a statute requiring pregnant married women to notify their husbands before engaging in conduct causing risk to the [fetal-being]. After all, if the husband's interest in the [fetal-being's] safety is sufficient predicate for state regulation, the State could reasonably conclude that pregnant wives should notify their husbands before drinking or smoking. (120 L. Ed. 2d 674 at 728)

In the Justices' plurality opinion, the potential loss of individual control over private moral choices inherent in spousal consent is clearly apparent. But Justices O'Connor, Kennedy, and Souter also invoked government's authority to take a moral position by noting that, at least from their perspective, "perhaps married women should notify their husbands before using contraceptives or before undergoing any type of surgery that may have complications affecting the husband's interest in his wife's reproductive organs" (120 L. Ed. 2d 674 at 728). Though the Justices made no direct comparison, consistency in their reasoning would require that the same conclusion be made about how a husband should approach his wife's interest in his "reproductive organ." Perhaps married men should notify their wives before undergoing a vasectomy, choosing a particular brand of condoms, or since different styles of underwear have been shown to affect sperm production, when choosing a particular type of underwear. Consistently applied or not, the point that Justices O'Connor, Kennedy, and Souter appear to be trying to convey is that while individuals "perhaps should" behave in a particular way when making procreative decisions with implications for other individuals, as autonomous moral agents they are free to choose not to behave in this way.

Beyond the point in the above discussion, recognizing the private nature of a woman acting in her capacity as an autonomous moral agent to choose abortion also can be understood as reflecting the Lockean prescription of religious tolerance. Government efforts to restrict or prohibit a woman from exercising the abortion decision almost always encompass some religious or theological position on when human life begins. But contrary to a government's endorsement and imposition of one theory of life onto the civic community, there has always been a "wide divergence of thinking on this most sensitive and difficult question" (*Roe* v. *Wade* 93 S. Ct. 705 at 730). Indeed, "the intensely divisive character of much of the national debate over the abortion issue reflects the deeply held religious convictions of many participants in the debate" as to when life begins (*Webster* v. *Reproductive Health Services* 106 L. Ed. 2d 410 at 470–Justice Stevens concurring in part and dissenting in part).

Thus, when government adopts a particular theological or moral position on when life begins and imposes that position upon members of the civil community who do not share this belief, government is failing both to recognize the competing moral beliefs on this question and to practice the religious/moral tolerance required of it by Lockean-styled liberalism. In brief, this Lockean prescription of religious tolerance means that government "may not adopt one theory of when life begins to justify its regulation of abortion" (*Akron* v. *Akron Center for Reproductive Health, Inc.* 76 L. Ed. 2d 687 at 713). For any theory of life it does adopt will be tantamount to "an unequivocal endorsement of a religious tenant of some but by no means all . . . [religious] faiths" (*Webster* v. *Reproductive Health Services* 106 L. Ed. 2d 410 at 467–Justice Stevens concurring in part and dissenting in part).

There is an important caveat, though, to this conclusion. As stated earlier in this discussion, Lockean-styled liberalism expects government to practice moral tolerance, but it does not require government to be completely indifferent to the moral choices made by the members of the civic community. Further, the requirement of moral tolerance is only a prescription against government using its authority and power to force or coerce private moral behavior that autonomous moral agents would not otherwise freely choose. The requirement does not prevent government from expressing a particular moral or theological point of view through actions directed at merely influencing private moral choices. If the Lockean prescription of moral tolerance extended to this realm of government action as well, then it would also be a prescription of moral indifference or neutrality. But to reiterate a point made in Chapter 2, government, like any individual member of the political community, "has the commission to admonish, exhort, convince another of error, and by reason draw him into truth" (*A Letter concerning Toleration*, 11). The Lockean requirement of moral tolerance, then, is only an expectation that government will communicate and promote its moral outlook through persuasion rather than the coercive power of law.

Beyond a Lockean expectation of religious tolerance, there remains to be discussed one more reason for recognizing the private nature of the abortion decision. Acknowledging the private moral choice of a woman to terminate an unwanted pregnancy through abortion is necessary to guarantee that women who chose to carry their pregnancies to full term also are free to do so without government interference. If the pro-life position against the private moral characteristic of the abortion decision and its push for government prohibition of abortion are carried to their logical ends, then the decision not to abort and to carry the fetal-being to term is no more private than the decision to abort. "If . . . the woman's interest in deciding whether to bear and beget a child [is not] recognized, [government] might as readily restrict a woman's rights to choose to carry a pregnancy to term as to terminate it, to further assert [government] interests in population control, or eugenics" (*Planned Parenthood of Southeastern Pennsylvania* v. *Casey* 120 L. Ed. f201 674 at 203).

For the reasons discussed above, then, it is possible to reasonably conclude that like the general liberty interest in procreative choice, the abortion decision must be recognized as both private and essential to a woman's self-preservation. As the Supreme Court correctly recognized in *Thornburgh* v. *American College of Obstetricians and Gynecologists* (90 L. Ed. 2d 779 at 801):

> Few decisions are more personal and intimate, more properly private, or more basic to individual dignity and autonomy, than a woman's decision . . . whether to end her pregnancy. A woman's right to make that choice freely is fundamental. Any other result . . . would protect inadequately a central part of the sphere of liberty that our law guarantees equally to all.

Concluding that a woman's liberty interest in the abortion decision is a private moral choice to be determined by a woman acting as an autonomous moral agent, prohibits government from imposing the political communities' moral view upon those women experiencing unwanted pregnancies. It is a recognition that no woman "should be compelled to surrender the freedom to make [the abortion] decision for herself simply because her 'value preferences' are not shared by the majority" (*Thornburgh* v. *American College of Obstetricians and Gynecologists* 90 L. Ed. 2d 779 at 804–Justice Stevens concurring). Rather, this conclusion acknowledges that "it is far better to permit some individuals to make incorrect decisions than to deny all individuals the right to make decisions that have a profound effect upon their destiny" (90 L. Ed. 2d 799 at 807–Justice Stevens concurring). This is the "prize and price" of liberty mentioned earlier, in Chapter 2. It requires that women who choose to terminate their unwanted pregnancies through abortion be given equal dignity and respect for their choices as the community gives to women who choose to carry their pregnancies to full term.

TO BE FREE FROM—
NOT ENTITLED TO

A woman's liberty interest in the abortion decision is to be free from government-forced or -coerced moral choices about how best to resolve her unwanted pregnancy, a choice without government intrusion into her private life. Defined in this manner, the abortion liberty, like all Lockean-informed liberty, is an expression of negative rather than positive freedom. As defined in Chapter 2, negative freedom means that individuals are free when government does not prohibit or place roadblocks in the way of their exercise of preexisting rights. It is not an entitlement to government assistance ensuring that individuals can fully exercise those rights (Glenn 1989, 188 fn. 2; Goldstein 1981, 335).

As an expression of negative freedom, a woman's liberty interest in the abortion decision only limits government from acting in ways to prohibit her private decision to chose whether or not to terminate an unwanted pregnancy by aborting the fetal-being (*Beal* v. *Doe* 97 S. S. Ct. 2366; *Harris* v. *McRae* 100 S. Ct. 2671; *Maher* v. *Roe* 97 S. Ct. 2376; *Poelker* v. *Doe* 97 S. Ct. 2391; *Rust* v. *Sullivan* 114 L. Ed. 2d 233; *Webster* v. *Reproductive Health Services* 106 L. Ed. 2d 410). It does not impose any positive obligation on government to secure for a woman the ability to actually exercise or act on her private moral choice to resolve her unwanted pregnancy through abortion. In practical terms, this recognition means that a Lockean-styled liberty interest in the abortion decision does not require government to provide a woman with the resources, facilities, or medical personnel necessary for performing either the elective or therapeutic abortion that a woman chooses to have (*Maher* v. *Roe* 97 S. Ct. 2376 at 2380; *Poelker* v. *Doe* 97 S. Ct. 2391 at 2392).

Yet nothing in Lockean-styled liberalism prohibits government from choosing the opposite course of action if it so desired and funding abortions and abortion-related services not just for women of poverty but for all women. Lockean-styled liberalism merely does not require it. It recognizes that "when an issue involves policy choices as sensitive as those implicated by the public funding of . . . abortion, the appropriate forum for their resolution . . . is the legislature" (*Maher* v. *Roe* 97 S. Ct. 2376 at 2385). If government chooses not to publicly fund abortion and abortion services, women of poverty remain "as before, . . . dependent on private sources for the service" they desire (*Maher* v. *Roe* 97 S. Ct. 2376 at 2383).

The pro-choice position generally refuses to recognize the negative characteristic of a woman's liberty interest in the abortion decision. Rather, advocates of this position argue that government has an affirmative and positive obligation to deliver to women of poverty the same access to abortion and abortion services as enjoyed by women of wealth (relatively speaking). These advocates interpret the Constitution as providing "remedies for every social and economic ill" confronting the nation (*Maher* v. *Roe* 97 S. Ct. 2376 at 2385). The positive freedom interpretation the pro-choice position gives to the Constitution is clearly evident in the sentiment expressed by Justice Blackmun in his dissenting opinion in *Beal*, *Maher* and *Poelker*:

> There is another world "out there," the existence of which the Court, I suspect, either chooses to ignore or fears to recognize. And so the cancer of poverty will continue to grow. This is a sad day for those who regard the Constitution as a force that would serve justice to all evenhandedly and in so doing, would better the lot of the poorest among us. (97 S. Ct. 2394 at 2399)

Believing as they do, pro-choice proponents of public funding routinely speak of government's "distressing insensitivity to the plight of impoverished pregnant women" (*Maher* v. *Roe* 97 S. Ct. 2376 at 2387–Justice Brennan dissenting). They act as if government purposely impoverishes these women and conspires to keep them in this condition. Thus, the pro-choice advocates deny "the private fact of indigency" (Goldstein 1981, 324). At the same time, they do not distinguish, in any Lockean manner, between an individual's inability to fully exercise protected liberty due to natural incapacities, such as a lack of intellectual or physical capability, and incapacities due to prohibited government interference. Thus, by failing to see and appreciate Locke's meaning of equality, his understanding of the roots of poverty, and the association between the two, they mistake Lockean equality for egalitarianism.

When Locke writes of equality, he has something very specific in mind. Working from the assumption that all individuals are "born to the same advantages of Nature" and with "the use of the same faculties," Locke teaches that everyone possesses an *equal right . . . to his [or her] Natural Freedom, without being subjected to the Will or the Authority of any other*" individual (*Second Treatise*, secs. 4, 54–emphasis in the original). In setting forth this assertion, Locke articulates a formal rather than a substantive or egalitarian understanding of equality. In fact, Locke generally can be understood as rejecting the notion that all individuals possess equal native capabilities, achieve equal results, or even an equal station in life. He writes:

> "I cannot be supposed to understand all sorts of *Equality*: *Age* or *Virtue* may give men a just Precedence: *Excellency of Parts and Merits* may place others above the Common Level: *Birth* may subject some, and the *Alliance* or *Benefits* others, to pay an *Observance* to those whom Nature, Gratitude or

other Respects may have made it due." (*Second Treatise*, sec. 54–emphasis in the original)

Expressed in this manner, Locke's understanding of an individual's natural equality in relationship to others recognizes and permits a great deal of personal inequality among individuals in most facets of their lives, resulting from: unequal natural capabilities; opportunities beyond their control, such as intellectual ability or their birth placement; or variation in individual industriousness and rationality. But while these personal inequalities may prevent substantive equality from occurring, they never justify the denial of formal equality. For Locke, all individuals, regardless of their personal inequalities, enjoy the formal equality to be free from the will or authority of any others regardless of the latter's superior abilities or higher station in life and to have the law of nature applied equally to all.

Locke's writings note that personal inequalities among individuals will be most readily apparent in their varying skills and abilities in acquiring property and wealth. According to Locke, an individual acquires property and wealth through the "*Labour* of his Body and the *Work* of his Hands" (*Second Treatise*, sec. 27–emphasis in the original). Those individuals who demonstrate themselves to be the most "Industrious and Rational" are most entitled to and likely to acquire property and wealth (*Second Treatise*, sec. 34). Therefore, it is among the least capable, least industrious, and the least rational members of the civil community that the roots of poverty are most likely to take hold in the sense that poverty is defined as the absence of sufficient enough property and wealth to secure one's own self-preservation.

Locke also recognizes that the unequal distribution of property and wealth between industrious and rational individuals and those least inclined is intensified by the "*Invention of Money* and the tacit Agreement of [individuals] to put a value on it" (*Second Treatise*, sec. 36–emphasis in the original). Through the invention of money, individuals change the source for the value of acquiring property from self-preservation, or what Locke refers to as the "*Conveniency of Life*," to value in more accumulation of property beyond what individuals need for their own use and survival (*Second Treatise*, sec. 36–emphasis in the original; see also secs. 31-34, 37-50). Locke writes that before the invention of money, property derived value only in regard to its usefulness to sustaining life, and the amount of property individuals could acquire was limited by nature to what they could use without spoilage. Beyond this point, the law of nature viewed the accumulation of property as an invasion of their neighbors' share (*Second Treatise*, secs. 31, 36). Since before the invention of money the right to acquire property was restricted to need, the unequal distribution of property between the industrious and rational and those less industrious and less rational was of minimal consequence.

The invention of money and the decision by members of the civil community to place a value on it fundamentally change the reason for accumulating property from preservation to wealth. The invention of money provides individuals with "some lasting thing that [they] might keep without spoiling, and that by mutual consent [they] would take in exchange for the truly useful, but perishable Supports of Life" (*Second Treatise*, sec. 47). The same variations in industriousness and rationality that accounted for individuals being more or less capable of accumulating property for their own preservation also has an impact on their ability to accumulate wealth.

But where the law of nature reasonably self-corrected these variations by limiting the accumulation of property to need, a Lockean-styled civil community has no analogous limitation or restriction on the accumulation of wealth. Instead, a Lockean-styled civil community institutionalizes variations in wealth. On this point, Locke notes that in consenting to bestow value on money, the civil community also is consenting to the "disproportionate and unequal Possession of the Earth" and an "inequality of private possessions" based upon personal inequalities in the industriousness and rationality of individuals (*Second Treatise*, sec. 50). By this consent, then, a Lockean civil community agrees to be inherently nonegalitarian and accepts that some of its members will be less well-off even residing in what today is called poverty.

Through the Constitution's incorporation of Lockean-styled liberalism, the same conclusion must be reached regarding this document: that it embodies a Lockean understanding of equality and inequality in property and wealth. For example, writing in defense of the newly proposed constitution and the government created by it, James Madison recognizes in *Federalist Paper 10* (124) "the diversity in the faculties of men, from which the right of property originates." Madison continues by noting: "The protection of these faculties is *the first object of government*. From the protection of *different and unequal faculties* of acquiring property, the possession of different degrees and kinds of property immediately results" (*Federalist Paper 10*, 124–emphasis added). Nor was Madison the only framer to express such sentiment. In his private notes regarding the debates that took place at the Constitutional Convention, Madison records Alexander Hamilton speaking in a vein similar to that which he himself expressed in *Federalist 10*. Madison reports Hamilton as recognizing that

nothing like an equality of property existed; that inequality would exist as long as liberty existed, and that it would unavoidably result from that very liberty itself. The inequality of property constituted the great and fundamental distinction in Society. When the Tribunal power has levelled the boundary between the *patricians and the plebeians* what followed? The distinction between rich and poor was substituted. (Ketcham 1986, 92)

If Madison and Hamilton's views are assumed to be representative of the framers, then the only possible conclusion is that the Constitution promotes a Lockean-styled understanding of equality. If this is true, the Constitution cannot be the egalitarian document many pro-choice supporters of public funding of abortion make it out to be.

In a Lockean-styled civil community that has chosen through consent to institutionalize substantive inequality in the accumulation of wealth, such as the one established by the Constitution, how is government to respond to this condition? The Lockean response, as Madison well noted, is for government to protect this unequal accumulation of property and wealth resulting from personal inequalities among members of the civil community. Lockean-styled government is under no obligation to eliminate these personal inequalities through any affirmative or positive action. Rather, its purpose remains, as in all manners concerning the private sphere, to secure for all individuals the freedom to acquire that level of wealth and private property that their natural abilities enable them to achieve. This means that government must ensure that individuals can accumulate wealth free from barriers erected by it or other members of the community.

But to reiterate a point made earlier, nothing in the minimal expectation that Lockean-styled liberalism has toward government prohibits it from assisting the least abled, least industrious, and least rational members of the civil community who fail on their own to acquire a sufficient level of wealth and property to secure their self-preservation. In fact, such actions would be in keeping with the Lockean notion of the public good and the continued survival of civil community. For if the least abled, industrious, and rational members of the community fail to secure sufficient wealth to provide for their self-preservation through the lawful application of their talents, then it is quite reasonable to assume that some of them may turn to unlawful means. When this occurs, no individual's property, wealth, or self-preservation is secure from invasion by the least fortunate segments of the community who by necessity are driven to reside outside its laws. Thus, to prevent or lessen this occurrence, Lockean-styled liberalism recognizes that the survival of the civil community and the security of all others' liberty make it prudent for government to assist the least capable, industrious, and rational members of the community to secure their self-preservation.

In applying an egalitarian/positive government misinterpretation of the Constitution to the abortion funding issue, pro-choice advocates further underscore their avoidance or lack of understanding of Lockean-styled liberalism by making an equal protection comparison between women of wealth and women of poverty when from a Lockean-derived understanding of equality none really exists. Inevitably, whenever the pro-choice position is thrust forth that government has an obligation to fund abortions for poor women, the justification is that to do otherwise violates the equal protection rights of women of poverty insofar as the absence of positive action on the part of government creates an arbitrary distinction between those women who can and cannot exercise their liberty interest in the abortion decision.

Laurence Tribe (1990, 207) articulates this position in his popular and widely read book *Abortion: The Clash of Absolutes*:

> Insofar as abortion itself remains legal, denying public funds for abortion is simply a collective decision that abortion be available to the rich and that abortion should remain . . . not just the woman's prerogative but the woman's problem. The denial to some women of the right to choose to terminate a pregnancy, while others can exercise that right freely . . . seems particularly immoral when the line between the two groups is based on something as unrelated to the situation of the pregnancy . . . and as frequently beyond a woman's control, as personal wealth.

Dissenting in *Beal* v. *Doe*, Justice Brennan expressed these same sentiments. He writes that the unwillingness of government to fund abortions or its direct prohibition of such funding results as a

> practical matter in forcing penniless pregnant women to have children they would not have borne if the [government] had not weighted the scales to make their choice to have abortions substantially more onerous. . . . "For a doctor who cannot afford to work for nothing, and a woman who cannot afford to pay him, . . . [government's] refusal to fund an abortion is as effective an 'interdiction' of it as would ever be necessary." (97 S. Ct. 2366 at 2376– quoting *Singleton* v. *Wulff* 428 U.S. 106 at 118-119)

To further bolster their equal protection argument, advocates of public funding also assert that the denial of such funds to women of poverty is even tantamount to racial discrimination, which is a more widely recognized basis for an equal protection claim against government. Justice Marshall writes that denying or prohibiting public funds for abortion falls "with great disparity upon women of minority races." He notes that "nonwhite women . . . obtain abortions at nearly twice the rate of whites and that almost 40 percent of minority women—more than five times the proportion of whites" are dependent upon government for their health care (*Beal* v. *Doe* 97 S. Ct. 2394 at 2397–Justice Marshall dissenting).

The egalitarian/positive freedom obligation supporters of public funding mistakenly impose upon government is clearly evident in the above examples. Like most pro-choice misconceptions about the public funding of abortion, this one, too, stems from the pro-choice disregard for the tradition of negative freedom associated with Lockean-styled liberalism, including its definition of equality. As discussed before, Lockean liberty is "to be free from something." It is not "to be entitled to something." Government must only refrain from acting against individuals applying their natural abilities to the exercise of their liberty. But it is not obligated to provide less able, less industrious, or less rational individuals with the means to exercise liberty at the same capacity as naturally superior individuals do—superior in the sense of being more able, more industrious, and more rational in maximizing access to liberty than their fellow members of the civil community. These inequalities are personal and not imposed by government. For Lockean-styled liberalism, these personal inequalities are and remain an everyday fact of life. Their existence and government toleration of them do not violate any Lockean understanding of equality either in nature or a civil community.

It is only when government chooses to go beyond the minimal expectations of Lockean-styled liberalism and provide individual members of the civil community with divisible and tangible services or benefits that it risks running afoul of Lockean-styled equality. In a civil community, one aspect of Lockean equality is the liberty to live under known and settled laws applied indifferently or equally to all members of the civil community at whom the laws are directed (*Second Treatise*, secs. 124, 125). Therefore, when government chooses to act positively and provide services to some part of the civil community, it is obligated to distribute those services indifferently among the individuals designated to receive them without regard to any such ascriptive characteristics as race or religion. Any violation of a Lockean-styled equality comes only when government services are not so distributed. Thus, in regard to government services and benefits, Lockean-styled equality requires a formal procedural comparison within the general classification of individuals at whom the services are directed (*Maher* v. *Roe* 97 S. Ct. 2376 at 2380). It is not concerned with a comparison between the designated benefactors of the government largesse and those who are not so designated.

It is with this understanding of equality and inequality that the public funding of abortion must be understood. When, in an effort to provide women of poverty some degree of health care, government adopts a program of funding selected medical services, it must do so in such a way that all who are eligible to receive those services do so in an impartial or indifferent manner. Lockean-styled equality exists when this is done. But if government stipulates that selected medical services are to be provided to all women of poverty, except those who are also women of color, Lockean-styled equality will not exist. The law is not being applied impartially or indifferently to the general class of individuals for which it was designed.

For the reasons spelled out in the above discussion, the decision by government not to fund abortions or abortion related services does not violate the equality of poor women for several reasons. First, when government decides to act positively and provide some medical services to women of poverty, it is acting in a way that Lockean-styled liberalism does not require it to do. It is acting merely on a prudent and charitable belief that providing those services is in the public interest. Second, since government is under no obligation to act in any positive manner toward individuals lacking the natural ability to act on their liberty, it in no way violates their liberty by refusing to fund services increasing the accessibility of otherwise less accessible liberty. Instead, the decision not to fund, as well as to fund, reflects government's chosen moral position and attempt at moral suasion.

Nor can a claim of government-imposed inequality between women of poverty and women of wealth exist when government chooses to provide some but not all medical procedures to poor women. Since Lockean-styled equality demands equality within a general classification and women of wealth reside outside that classification, there can be no government-imposed inequality between those two groups. Government-imposed inequality would exist only if government discriminated among poor women. As long as all women of poverty are denied access to abortion and abortion-related services, Lockean-styled equality is maintained.

Indeed, if the pro-choice position that government recognition of varying levels of economic status among individuals is constitutionally valid, then carried to its logical extreme government would be greatly hampered in providing any social-welfare services to the poor, including abortion funding. Under the logic of the pro-choice position, government would be prohibited from providing these benefits without also providing analogous services to everyone regardless of economic standing. To do less would cause an unacceptable inequality—unacceptable, that is, if consistency is an important element in one's philosophy. For according to the egalitarian logic of the pro-choice position, when government funds access to a protected liberty for the poor, it reduces the cost of exercising that liberty to zero. For example, abortion funding for poor women reduces the cost of exercising the liberty interest in the abortion decision for women of poverty to zero. But for women of wealth, the cost of exercising the abortion liberty remains the going market price. Thus, by funding abortions for only the less or least well-off women in a political community, government creates an economic inequality for all the rest who must pay the market price.

Consider, then, the extent to which the pro-choice perspective's egalitarian/positive misinterpretation of the Constitution would have to be extended in order to be constitutionally consistent. It would appear that if the Constitution requires egalitarian and positive action on the part of government to guarantee indigent women access to abortion and abortion services, similar actions to secure other liberty interests less fully exercised because of economic circumstances would also be required (Schulte 1975, 5). For example, the constitutionally protected right to privacy allows individuals to read pornography in the freedom of their homes. But no one would seriously argue that the government is obligated to provide impoverished individuals with a readily available supply of pornographic materials so that they can exercise this liberty interest to the fullest (Goldstein 1981, 320).

Similarly, under the Constitution, individuals enjoy the freedom of speech. During election years, many individuals exercise this liberty in support of some candidates and in opposition to others. But individuals of greater wealth may contribute large sums of money to their favorite candidates or political parties. Some even are able pay for television commercials to express their opposition to particular candidates. These individuals clearly are more fully able to exercise their freedom of expression than persons of lesser means who find themselves limited in their expression to placing a candidate's placard on their front lawns. But no one would seriously contend that the Constitution requires government to provide these less well-off individuals with public funds so that they can exercise their liberty interest in speech at the same level as wealthy individuals.

Thus, the egalitarian/positive obligation pro-choice proponents of public spending would mistakenly impose on government as a constitutional obligation appears quite ludicrous when thoughtfully considered. To hold as the pro-choice position does that government must provide women of poverty equal access to abortion "would mark a drastic change in our understanding of the Constitution" (*Harris* v. *McRae* 65 L. Ed. 2d 784 at 805). It would be a change with absolutely no grounding in the Lockean-styled liberalism so important to the creation of the Constitution. Indeed, this position would actually negate important Lockean precepts, including the Lockean prescription of moral tolerance without moral indifference.

As already noted earlier in this chapter, Lockean-styled government must tolerate the private moral choice that some women make to resolve their unwanted pregnancies through abortion. But it is not required to practice moral indifference to abortion. Lockean-styled government is free to try to persuade women to its moral position as long as government does not seek influence through prohibiting or coercing their choice. Yet by requiring government to guarantee equal access to abortion and abortion-related services, the egalitarian/positive obligation that the pro-choice position would impose on government denies that government can practice anything but moral indifference. This insistence on moral indifference inherent in the pro-choice position's support for public funding of abortions is keenly illustrated in the opinion of the three-judge United States District Court striking down as unconstitutional a Connecticut statute that excluded nontheraputic abortions from the state's medical assistance program: "The state may not justify its refusal to pay for one type of expense arising from pregnancy on the basis that it morally opposes such an expenditure of money" (*Maher* v. *Roe* 97 S. Ct. 2376 at 2379-2380–quoting 408 F. Supp. 660 at 664).

Admittedly, this discussion about public funding of abortion appears insensitive to the plight of women of poverty who experience unwanted pregnancies. It is possible, though, to conclude the constitutional correctness of this position and still not agree that government's unwillingness to assist women of poverty in exercising their liberty interest in the abortion decision is "good" public policy. Indeed, the opposite is probably truer; in many instances, the prohibition of public funds for abortion and abortion-related services will be detrimental to those women of poverty denied these services. Though it is possible to disagree with the policy implications of the negative nature of a woman's liberty interest in the abortion decision, the understanding of Lockean liberalism thus far articulated and the Constitution's own indebtedness to this theory of government do not appear to allow for any other logical conclusion. Public funding of abortions and abortion-related services, while constitutionally permissible, is not constitutionally required. To conclude otherwise, individuals would have to read their own social and economic theory into the document. Recalling Justice Holmes' admonishment to the Court in *Lochner* v. *New York* (198 U.S. 45), this is something individuals should be unwilling to do.

In *Lochner*, Justice Holmes, reacting to the Court majority's attempt to read laissez-faire capitalism into the Constitution, strongly admonished his brethren by correctly observing that the "Constitution is not intended to embody a particular economic theory" (O'Brien 1991, 253). Filled with the good intention of eliminating an inequitable situation for indigent women, those individuals who incorrectly impose a positive reading onto the Constitution would likewise read their own economic and social theory into the Constitution. But rather than the laissez-faire capitalism rebuked by Justice Holmes, proponents of public funding for abortions and abortion-related services would read the social-economic theory of the welfare state into the Constitution. But the Constitution today no more enacts Michael Harrington's *The Other America* than it did Herbert Spencer's *Social Statistics* during the days of Justice Holmes.

GOVERNMENT'S INFLUENCE
ON THE ABORTION DECISION

It is clear from the above discussion that both abortion and the broader liberty interest in procreation are, and must be, in the private sphere of human life. Assigning the abortion decision to the private sphere effectively means that government cannot forcibly impose its idea of correct moral behavior on women considering abortion. Instead, the private nature of the abortion decision requires government to tolerate abortion and be pro-choice insofar as pro-choice means prohibiting governmental interference designed to coerce women into not having abortions or to impose an outright ban on abortion. As with other liberty interests, government's responsibility in regard to abortion is to protect this liberty so that women can act as autonomous moral agents when deciding how best to resolve an unwanted pregnancy.

But despite the pro-choice position required by Lockean-styled liberalism, government can still legitimately seek to influence through noncoercive means the private choices women make regarding the resolution of unwanted pregnancies. Indeed, the whole point about moral tolerance without moral indifference is that government, too, is permitted to make choices about what is correct moral behavior and to attempt to influence members of the civil community to accept its position and behave accordingly. Therefore, from a Lockean understanding, government possesses the discretion to decide whether it will be more pro-choice than minimally required or whether it will merely retain this minimal requirement and actively pursue permissible anti-abortion activities. For example, to be more actively pro-choice than Lockean-styled liberalism requires, government could "constitutionally declare that . . . it will pay the full cost of abortions for all pregnant women eligible for Medicaid, but that Medicaid will no longer pay any cost related to childbirth" (Goldstein 1981, 317).

Or government could maintain only the minimally required pro-choice protection and pursue an aggressive anti-abortion position so long as its actions were directed merely at influencing and not coercing or prohibiting a woman's private decision whether or not to abort the fetal-being. As the discussion on public funding highlights, one way in which this influence can take place is through funding programs that promote the government's position and not funding those that do not. Chief Justice

Rehnquist expressed these same sentiments in *Rust* v. *Sullivan* (114 Ed. 2d 233 at 255):

> The Government can, without violating the Constitution, selectively fund a program to encourage certain activities it believes to be in the public interest, without at the same time funding an alternative program which seeks to deal with problems in another way. In so doing, the Government has not discriminated on the basis of viewpoint; it has merely chosen to fund [and promote] one activity to the exclusion of the other.

Properly understood, then, the Constitution, with its Lockean-inspired foundation, "implies no limitation on the authority of [government] to make a value judgment favoring childbirth over abortion, and to implement that judgment" by designing programs to influence the decisions women make regarding abortion (*Maher* v. *Roe* 97 S. Ct. 2376 at 2382). When government chooses to promote alternatives to unwanted pregnancies other than abortion, it places no governmental obstacle in the path of a woman who chooses to ignore governmental influence and still invoke her private decision to abort the fetal-being (*Harris* v. *McRae* 448 U.S. 297 at 315). Rather, it only promotes alternative choices that it believes may be in the best interest of the political community and of the women confronting the abortion decision (*Harris* v. *McRae* 448 U.S. 297 at 315).

It would appear, then, that government possesses a great deal of leeway in how it chooses to go about pursuing an anti-abortion position, if it prefers this policy course. But explicit in the foregoing discussion is the standard by which government's anti-abortion activities must be judged. The Lockean prescription of moral tolerance without moral indifference is that standard. This prescription imposes a balance upon any government action designed to discourage the incident of abortion. It requires that government address both the substance of the moral behavior it is pursuing and the means chosen to promote it and to encourage individuals to practice it.

The Lockean expectation of moral tolerance without moral indifference dictates that all government anti-abortion activities (as well as its pro-choice activities, for that matter) be "calculated" to *inform* [a] woman's free choice [and] not to hinder it" (*Planned Parenthood of Southeastern Pennsylvania* v. *Casey* 120 L. Ed. 2d 674 at 715—emphasis added). Therefore, when government embraces an anti-abortion morality, it must ask itself whether the means chosen for implementing this morality coerce women to carry the fetal-being full term rather than terminate unwanted pregnancies through abortion. If government answers yes to this question, it cannot go forward with its anti-abortion policy as formulated. Such coercive action would "place a substantial obstacle in the path of a woman seeking an abortion" (120 L. Ed. 674 at 714). Government, therefore, must find a noncoercive way to achieve its anti-abortion morality that does not sacrifice the moral tolerance required of it by Lockean-styled liberalism. Thus, proposed anti-abortion actions that are not tempered with sufficient moral tolerance to allow women to remain free in their private moral choice surrounding the decision whether or not to abort unwanted pregnancies are constitutionally impermissible.

Under this Lockean-inspired standard, some goals and actions adopted by government to pursue an anti-abortion morality are *prima facie* invalid. For example, spousal consent, already noted as being impermissible because it temporarily places a woman in involuntary servitude, is also *prima facie* invalid because the very act of requiring an adult woman to seek the consent of her spouse before exercising her liberty interest in abortion lacks moral tolerance. Spousal notification enables her husband to impose his moral position upon her. Also under this Lockean-inspired standard, some broad anti-abortion goals of government generally will be constitutionally permissible but some of the alternative means by which these goals can be pursued will not be. For instance, the anti-abortion goal behind the United States Department of Health and Human Services' regulations banning abortion counseling in programs receiving Title X funds under the Public Health Service Act upheld in *Rust* v. *Sullivan* (114 L. Ed. 2d 233 at 247), would not be constitutionally permissible. The department's decision to promote an anti-abortion morality was clearly permissible under Lockean-styled liberalism. In addition, as the previous decision on public funding underscores, the prohibition on the use of Title X monies to fund abortion counseling and record-keeping procedures to guarantee Title X funds were kept separate, were permissible ways of expressing the government's preferred morality of childbirth over abortion. But the regulations also required that when a client specifically requested abortion information, family planning clinics receiving Title X funds were supposed to offer a response, such as the clinic "does not consider abortion an appropriate method of family planning and therefore does not counsel or refer for abortion" (*Rust* v. *Sullivan* 114 L. Ed. 2d 233 at 247–quoting CFR sec. 59.8(b)(5).) It was here at the point of requiring family planning clinics to expressly disavow abortion as an acceptable way of resolving unwanted pregnancies that the Health and Human Services's regulations crossed the line between informing and hindering a woman's free choice, and therefore became coercive rather than merely influential. By removing important and relevant information from women dependent on Title X-funded health clinics, these regulations clearly advanced the department's anti-abortion position.

But in requiring Title X family planning clinics to completely disavow abortion as a form of family planning, the department chose a course of action that intentionally attempted to hinder rather than inform a woman's free choice about abortion. It did so by requiring information necessary for making a well-thought-out choice as to how to resolve an unwanted pregnancy to be deliberately and intentionally withheld. In forcing family planning agencies to disavow abortion, the Department of Health and Human Services's actions were knowingly designed to place a substantial obstacle in the way of women seeking family planning information. This deliberate denial of information was intended to coerce rather than merely influence women into foregoing abortions and carrying the fetal-beings to full term. In so doing, the Department failed to pursue its moral position on abortion with the sufficient moral tolerance required by Lockean-styled liberalism. Justice Blackmun echoed these same sentiments in his *Rust* dissent:

> The [woman's] right of self-decision can be effectively exercised only if [she] possesses enough information to enable an intelligent choice. . . . By suppressing medically pertinent information and injecting a restrictive ideological message unrelated to consideration of [her] health, the Government places formidable obstacles in the path of Title X clients' freedom of choice. . . . Both the purpose and the result of the challenged Regulations is to deny women the ability voluntarily to decide their procreation destiny. For these women, the Government will have obliterated the freedom to choose as surely as if it banned abortions outright. The denial of this freedom is . . . a consequence . . . of Government's ill-intentioned distortion of the information it has chosen to provide. (*Rust* v. *Sullivan* 114 L. Ed. 2d 233 at 271)

It is worth noting that had it so desired, the Department of Health and Human Services could have formulated regulations that were faithful to the Lockean standard of moral tolerance without moral indifference, thereby still pursuing its anti-abortion morality in a constitutionally correct manner. To accomplish this, the Title X regulation would have had to be formulated to merely require that the government's anti-abortion position be among the information presented to women seeking abortion counseling and have its position clearly labeled as such. Such regulations would not have had the intention of deliberately misleading women seeking family planning counseling into believing that the anti-abortion position was the clinics' position and not among the choices they could consider in resolving an unwanted pregnancy. Rather, the government's anti-abortion position merely would have been one of several views included among the information these women received. They, then, would have been free to accept or reject the government's position in their attempts to make informed decisions on how to exercise their liberty interest in the abortion decision.

An even clearer example of permissible goals likely being carried out through impermissible means is the issue of informed consent. In the abstract, informed consent reflects a concern that before a woman exercises her private moral choice regarding the abortion decision, that she possesses "all relevant information regarding [her] condition and alternative treatments, including possible benefits, risks, costs, and other consequences, and significant uncertainties surrounding any of this information" (*The President's Commission for the Study of Ethical Problems in Medicine and Biomedical and Behavioral Research* 1982, 2). It is a concern that before a woman executes the abortion decision she engages in as reasoned a consideration of its medical implications as she is capable of doing.

The requirement of informed consent is consistent with the Lockean values of self-determination over private moral choices, self-preservation, reason, and the government's obligation to protect individuals in their self-preservation. For these reasons, then, when informed consent is designed to secure individual self-preservation for a woman through a well-reasoned choice, informed consent laws "may be assured, constitutionally, . . . to the extent of requiring her . . . written consent" before undergoing an abortion (*Planned Parenthood of Central Missouri* v. *Danforth* 96 S. Ct. 2831 at 2840). But the pursuit of legally enforceable consent is limited to the medical implications of abortion. "The validity of an informed consent requirement . . . rests on [government's] interest in protecting the health [thus the preservation] of the pregnant woman" (*Akron* v. *Akron Center for Reproductive Health* 76 L. Ed. 2d 687 at 711). It does not extend to the legally required and enforceable informed consent of the government's moral position on abortion. To allow otherwise would be to violate the Lockean standard of moral tolerance without moral indifference.

Forced receipt by women exercising their liberty interest in the abortion decision of information pertaining to the government's moral position on abortion, particularly information with which they do not agree, clearly ignores the Lockean concern for moral tolerance. Therefore, government lacks absolute authority to decide carte blanche what information a woman must have and consider before voluntarily consenting to an abortion. Government is restricted to requiring only information that is medically necessary for a woman to make an informed and reasoned choice about whether or not to consent to an abortion. It cannot require information designed to dissuade a woman from exercising her choice according to her own moral dictates (*Akron* v. *Akron Center for Reproductive Health* 76 L. Ed. 2d 687 at 711-712; *Thornburgh* v. *American College of Obstetricians and Gynecologists* 90 L. Ed. 2d 779 at 794).

Under this standard, then, government may require that a physician or other health-care provider inform a woman considering an abortion about the physical and psychological complications she may experience during and after an abortion. For example, the following provision from the Akron city ordinance on the regulation of abortion declared constitutionally invalid by the Supreme Court in 1983 would seem to appear constitutionally permissible if a Lockean understanding of the abortion liberty were practiced and if the information were medically correct:

> That abortion is a major surgical procedure which can result in serious complications, including hemorrhage, perforated uterus, infection, menstrual disturbances, sterility and miscarriage and prematurity in subsequent pregnancies; and that abortion may leave essentially unaffected or may worsen any existing psychological problems she may have, and can result in severe emotional disturbances. (*Akron* v. *Akron Center for Reproductive Health* 76 L. Ed. 2d 687 at 698 fn. 5)

But under the Lockean standard articulated in this discussion, government cannot require information to be presented to a woman considering abortion that addresses morally charged issues such as when life begins, the legal obligation of the fetal-being's biological father to support it if a full-term pregnancy is carried out, alternatives to abortions, and public and private agencies available to assist the pregnant woman if she chooses not to terminate her pregnancy. The forced receipt or awareness of the availability of this information imposes too directly upon the pregnant woman the government's moral opposition to abortion. It speaks both of government's moral intolerance rather than its tolerance and speaks of government's misguided efforts to coerce rather than influence correct moral behavior.

In addition, the messenger chosen by the government to deliver its anti-abortion morality to women considering abortion is suspect. Most informed consent statutes make the attending physician or some other health-care provider deliver the government's anti-abortion message inherent in nonmedical information. In so doing, government makes these individuals its agents in the delivery of a moral position and message with which they may not agree (*Thornburgh* v. *American College of Obstetricians and Gynecologists* 90 L. Ed. 2d 779 at 795). But from a Lockean perspective, government can no more require one private individual to convey its moral position to another private individual than it can force individuals exercising private choices to behave in ways it deems morally correct. To do so violates those individuals' liberty as private, autonomous moral agents.

In addition, the forced conveyance of the government's moral position by physicians and other health care providers—backed up with legal sanctions against reluctant messengers—intrudes upon their liberty to acquire wealth and property through the exercise of a chosen legal occupation. The nonmedical aspects of informed consent forces these individuals to choose between exercising their private moral outlook in conflict with the government's officially chosen one, or continuing in their chosen profession at the cost of sacrificing their private beliefs. Since under the Lockean standard of moral tolerance without moral indifference government cannot force either receipt of information onto women or a reluctant third party to be its agent, government must address its concern for morally informed consent in the same manner through which it must pursue any of its anti-abortion morality: that is, through noncoercive means. This approach may consist of a wide array of activities, such as public service campaigns expressing government's perceived immorality of abortion or funding anti-abortion counseling.

The Lockean standard of moral tolerance without moral indifference may restrict government to promoting informed consent on the medical implications of abortion. But what a Lockean understanding of medical implications means may be broader than that traditionally associated with a pro-choice position. It includes receipt of information pertinent to the medical implications of the abortion for the fetal-being at that point in its development. Under this broad notion of medical implication, then, it would be permissible for government to require that before consenting to an abortion a woman be informed of such factors as the possible viability of the fetal-being; the extent of brain, heart, and lung functions; and the fetal-being's likely sensibility to pain.

As later discussed in detail in Chapter 6, government possesses an interest in the potential viable and independent life of the fetal-being. For the moment, though, it must suffice to observe that the government's interest in the fetal-being stems from a Lockean recognition that it has an obligation to see that individuals do not exercise their liberty in ways harmful to others. As it applies to the fetal-being, this obligation grows in intensity until viability, at which time under most circumstances it supersedes a woman's liberty interest in the abortion decision.

Thus, legally mandating that a woman considering an abortion be informed as to its medical implication for the fetal-being appears a reasonable way of sensitizing her to the recognition that she cannot be isolated in her liberty interest in the abortion decision (*Roe* v. *Wade* 93 S. Ct. 705 at 730). It may underscore for her that for her to be free to exercise her private choice requires that the developing life of the fetal-being, whatever that life may be, be terminated. It would allow her the opportunity to decide for herself if the choice to exercise her liberty interest in the abortion decision should be mitigated in any way by the harm done to the fetal-being.

Another popular restriction associated with informed consent, the twenty-four-hour waiting period, also runs afoul of Lockean-styled liberalism. First, allowing a waiting period before the exercise of the liberty interest in an abortion decision without also allowing government-mandated waiting periods before the exercise of other liberty interests is inherently contradictory to the Lockean distinction between the public and private sphere of human existence. If government possesses the authority to invade the private sphere to impose a waiting period on the exercise of the abortion liberty, then it must also be able to impose waiting periods on the exercise of such other liberty interests as which church to be baptized into, where to live, and whom to marry. Few individuals, though, would accept such invasion into these private decisions.

Second, as has been repeatedly stressed in this chapter, government need not take any positive action to provide members of the civil community with resources necessary for exercising liberty beyond the point which they are naturally capable of doing. But neither may government take positive action intended to make more difficult for members of the civil community the exercise of their liberty, that may result from private decisions it opposes. To be so allowed would be to violate the Lockean purpose for government, that being to secure liberty. By this standard, then, any government-imposed waiting period before a woman may exercise her liberty interest in the abortion decision is impermissible. On the pretense of fostering informed consent, government, through the adoption of a waiting period, knowingly and willingly imposes its moral position on some women by increasing their monetary cost of securing access to an abortion.

Moreover, waiting periods also do violence to the Lockean understanding of equality. As noted earlier in this chapter, a Lockean equality assumes all normal adult individuals possess the use of the same reasoning faculties. This assumption is the basis for all individuals possessing equal rights. But the imposition on women of a waiting period before they can make an important decision on how to best exercise their procreative liberty where no similar restriction is imposed on men's exercise of their procreative liberty violates this assumption of equal access to reasoning capabilities. Such a state-imposed waiting period rests on an "outmoded and unacceptable assumption about the decision making capacity of women" (*Planned Parenthood of Southeastern Pennsylvania* v. *Casey* 120 L. Ed. 2d 674 at 742–Justice Stevens concurring in part and dissenting in part). In short, any government-imposed waiting period rests on the assumption that women lack the same capacity as men in making reasoned medical and moral choices about how best to exercise their procreative liberty and, therefore, government must provide them with medical and moral direction in these matters. It treats normal adult women as if they are still children and have not yet reached an age of maturity where the reasoning capacity can be reasonably assumed. This last point is more fully developed in Chapter 5 and its analysis of minor women's access to abortion.

5

The Abortion Decision and Minor Women

In a *Time* magazine cover story entitled "Abortion's Hardest Cases," reporter Margaret Carlson (July 9, 1990, 24) writes that in regard to abortion a better world would be one "in which children too young to understand the power of sex did not engage in it" and those "unprepared to be pregnant did not become so." To this, she might easily have added that this world also would be one in which if minor women became pregnant, they would feel able to seek the counsel of their parents who, in turn, would guide them, without moral judgment or condemnation, toward the "best" resolution of their unwanted pregnancies whether that be abortion, adoption, or parenthood.

But this "better world" does not exist. Unwanted pregnancies among teenage women have reached epidemic proportions (Henshaw et al. 1989; Singh 1986; Trussell 1988). These pregnancies, in turn, account for one out of every four abortions performed in the United States (Information Aids, Inc. 1988, 42). Yet, minor women seeking abortions are likely to encounter opposition or impediments to their decisions from the public, their parents, and government. Public opinion polls show that an overwhelming majority of the adult population believes that having an abortion is among those things teenage women should not be able to do without parental consent. In addition, the majority of adults favor laws that require teenage women to receive this consent prior to having an abortion. A large majority of the public also would encourage their teenage daughters, if they were to become pregnant, to raise the child alone, place the child for adoption, or marry the father before they would advise abortion (Carlson, July 9, 1990, 22-25).

In the matter of teenage abortions, government policy generally reflects this public and parental opposition. Two-thirds of the fifty states have either parental consent or notification laws (Carlson July 9, 1990, 23; Samborn December 4, 1989, 39). In the post-*Webster* and *Casey* era, these laws are among the "growth industries" in anti-abortion legislation and are debated more often than any other kind of abortion restrictions. In 1990, more than seventy pieces of parental consent or notification legislation were introduced in twenty-five state legislatures (Allan Guttmacher Institute December 1990, iv). In 1991, more than forty new parental consent or notification bills were proposed in twenty-two state legislatures (Allan Guttmacher Institute December 1991, iv).

Though widespread opposition to teenage access to abortion exists, important questions remain unresolved. Is it a legitimate exercise of either parental or state authority to choose for teenage women experiencing unwanted pregnancies how these pregnancies are to be resolved? Or, do teenage women possess a liberty interest in procreative decisions, such as whether to conceive or not or, if unwanted conception occurs, whether to abort the fetal-being or not? If so, is this liberty the equivalent of the procreative liberty enjoyed by adult women? Or, does their status as minor women somehow limit their procreative liberty? As with the general liberty interest in the abortion decision, Locke's liberalism also can be applied to these questions concerning minor women's access to abortion. A Lockean analysis of these questions can clarify the liberty minor women enjoy or do not enjoy; the nature of parental authority over minor women; and the role of government in protecting both the interest of minor women and parents and maintaining the delicate balance between the two.

LIBERTY AND THE LOCKEAN CHILD

In articulating the liberty enjoyed by children, Locke writes that children are not born in a full state of equality "though they are born to it" (*Second Treatise*, sec. 55). To be in a full state of equality or liberty requires that individuals have both a knowledge and understanding of the "Law of Reason" by which natural rights and laws become known (*Second Treatise*, sec. 57). For Locke, reason is "the distinctive human faculty for self-preservation" (Tarcov 1984, 72). It is the "Voice of God" within individuals directing them toward those actions that promote their self-preservation and away from their self-destruction (*First Treatise*, sec. 86; see also Prangle 1988, 172-243).

Through reason, individuals are able to know and understand the limits imposed upon their liberty by the law of nature (*Second Treatise*, sec. 63). Knowing these limits on liberty, in turn, promotes self-preservation, thereby enabling individuals to better enjoy liberty. Locke writes:

> For *Law* in its true Notion, is not so much the Limitation as *the direction of a free and intelligent Agent* to his proper Interest, and prescribes no farther than is for the general Good of those under the Law. . . . *[The] end of the Law* is not to abolish or restrain, but *to preserve and enlarge Freedom*. (*Second Treatise*, sec. 57–emphasis in the original)

But, according to Locke, the only individual to have ever been "born" to a full state of equality knowing reason, thereby also knowing the means to his own self-preservation, was Adam. Locke writes that Adam was created the "perfect Man" with a body and mind in "full possession of their Strength and Reason." He was, therefore, capable from "the first Instant of his being to . . . govern his Actions according to the Dictates of the Law of Reason which God had implanted in him" for the purpose of securing his self-preservation (*Second Treatise*, sec. 56).

But Adam's children, and all who have come since, having entered the world through natural birth rather than divine creation, have not had the law of reason implanted in them from the "first instant" of their lives. Instead, natural birth produces children who are "weak and helpless, without Knowledge or Understanding" and "without the use of Reason" (*Second Treatise*, secs. 56, 57). Because children are born in this manner— without knowledge of how to secure their own self-preservation—they cannot be under the law of reason and, therefore, cannot belong to the full state of liberty and equality. Locke expresses this point when he writes: "[N]o Body can be under a law, which is not promulgated to him; and this Law being promulgated or made known by *Reason* only, he that is not come to the Use of his Reason, cannot be said to be *under this Law*" (*Second Treatise*, sec. 57–emphasis in the original).

To recognize and accept, as Locke did, that children are born without reason and, therefore, are not in a full state of equality does not mean that children possess no liberty. They do, but in a greatly diminished scope. Despite the absence of reason, Locke recognizes that children still possess liberty interests in preservation, nourishment, and education. (*First Treatise*, sec. 89; see also Lamprecht 1962, 126; Tarcov 1984, 67-68; Yolton 1985, 37). Children possess these three liberty interests, in part, because they are all necessary for bringing them to reason (*First Treatise*, sec. 89).

This justification for what liberty children do possess is important because it is at the state of reason that children quit being outside the full state of equality and enter into it. At the state of reason, children are presumed to possess sufficient "experience, perspective, and judgment to recognize and avoid choices that could be detrimental" to their or others' preservation (*Bellotti* v. *Baird*, 99 S. Ct. 3035 at 3043). At this point, they are presumed to know the law of reason and the limit it imposes on their liberty (*Second Treatise*, sec. 59).

But before children arrive at this state, Locke recognizes that parents or somebody else, "who [are] presumed to know how far the Law [of reason] allows a Liberty," must "understand for [their children], . . . will for [them], . . . and regulate [their] Actions" (*Second Treatise*, secs. 58, 59). Through this parental control and guidance, children also become free to enjoy additional liberty. Locke writes: "A *Child* is *Free* by his *Father's Title*, by his *Father's Understanding*, which is to govern him, till he hath it of his own" (*Second Treatise*, sec. 61–emphasis in the original).

Locke writes further that during the period when children lack reasoning of their own, parents have a special obligation to inform their children's minds, and to move them toward the state of maturity or reason (*Second Treatise*, sec. 58). The first part of this parental duty is education, and Locke is very clear as to about what children are to be taught in order to learn the law of reason. In preparing their children for the state of reason, Locke specifically instructs parents to educate both the body and mind of their children. He writes:

> A Sound Mind in a Sound Body, is a short, but full Description of a Happy State in this World; He that has these Two, has little more to wish for; and he that wants either of them, will be but little the better for anything else. (*Some Thoughts Concerning Education*, sec. 1)

Locke goes on to recommend that parents instruct their children in the *"Preservation and Improvement of a Healthy,* or at least, *not sickly Constitution"* (*Some Thoughts Concerning Education*, sec. 4–emphasis in the original). Locke writes that when parents educate their children's minds, their principal business is "to set the Mind right, that on all Occasions it may dispose to consent to nothing, but what may be suitable to the Dignity and Excellency of a rational creature" (*Some Thoughts Concerning Education*, sec. 32).

In discussing the nature of parental authority, Locke explicitly recognizes that parents serve as a temporary government over their children. Locke writes that in this role, parents "have a sort of rule and jurisdiction over [their children], when they come into the world, and for some time after" (*Second Treatise*, sec. 55). But the temporary government of parental authority under which children reside is unlike the government under which their parents live (*Second Treatise*, sec. 67). The most notable distinction is the different justifications on which parental authority and government are based. Government secures liberty for all adult individuals possessing the power to reason. It is based upon consent.

In contrast, children, not being born to reason, lack the capacity to freely consent. They "lack the developmental skills necessary for avoiding choices harmful to them." Thus, during their infancy and youthful years, children are unable to adequately care for themselves. Accordingly, the temporary government of parental authority, therefore, derives "from [this] duty which is incumbent upon [the parents], to take care of their offspring, during the imperfect state of childhood . . . to inform [children's] minds, and govern the actions of their yet ignorant nonage, till reason shall take its place" (*Second Treatise*, sec. 58) and the "ultimate goal of . . . independence and adulthood" is achieved (Keiter 1982, 507).

Though civic government and parental government are premised upon different needs, Locke recognizes that the temporary government of parental authority is very much like civil government in one important aspect. Parental authority, like civic government, is limited by the law of nature. As such, it can never be absolute. Parental authority can never extend to the power of "life and death, at any time, over their children" (*Second Treatise*, sec. 170). Rather, it is limited to "the Help, Instruction and Preservation of their offspring" (*Second Treatise*, sec. 170). Indeed, these obligations are "so incumbent on parents for their children's good, that nothing can absolve them from taking care of [their children]" (*Second Treatise*, sec. 67).

Failure to abide by these limits means that parents can forfeit their authority over their children. Parents who "quit" the care of their children actually lose their "power over them" (*Second Treatise*, sec. 65). Locke does not expressly say who determines when parents have forfeited or quit their authority over their children. Nor does he say to whom this authority is transferred. Nevertheless, Locke does recognize some notion of forfeiture and transfer. For example, he writes that parental authority "belongs as much to the *foster-father* of an exposed child, as to the natural father of another" (*Second Treatise*, sec. 65–emphasis in the original).

Though Locke is fairly silent on this point, it is logical to conclude that the responsibility for determining forfeiture and transfer of parental power rests with the government of the political community to which the parents are members. As noted in Chapter 2, in a political community, adult members surrender to government their authority in a state of nature to judge and punish individuals who invade and violate their natural rights. They do so to better protect and secure their natural rights. It seems logical, then, that government should provide children with an analogous protection from parental abuse. To deny children this protection would leave them in an unsecured state far worse than that in which adult individuals found themselves before forming a political community. It would be a state where parental authority would be absolute and arbitrary.

ENTRY INTO A FULL
STATE OF EQUALITY

Reaching the state of reason is the doorway through which children pass from the jurisdiction of their parents' temporary government over them and enter into the full state of equality. But Locke does not require perfect reason before the state of full liberty can be entered into. Children need only to know the law of reason as "well as several others, who live, as Freemen, under the Law" (*Second Treatise*, sec. 170). In fact, Locke proposes no real test to determine whether children actually know the law of reason and its instructions for self-preservation and the preservation of others. As a prerequisite for liberty, then, reason is a relative condition dependent upon the independent capability of individuals in comparison to others, rather than some absolute measure (Tarcov 1984, 72).

Reason may free children to enter the full state of equality but a question remains as to when children actually reach this state. Quoting Richard Hooker, Locke (*Second Treatise*, sec. 61–emphasis in the original) asks: "*But at what time . . . a Man may be said to have attain'd so far forth the use of Reason* [?]" At some specific age, appears to be the answer to this question. But Locke's answer underscores the inherent difficulty in determining the precise age when children are sufficiently mature to know reason and govern themselves according to reason's law (Yolton 1985, 37). Again quoting Hooker, Locke replies that the age at which children achieve reason is more easily determined by common sense than by any "*Skill or Learning*" (*Second Treatise*, sec. 61–emphasis in the original). One common sense criterion Locke employs to determine the age at which reason occurs is to presume that children have reached this state at least at the age at which their parents were so presumed to have reached it:

Is a Man under the Law of *England*? *What made him free* of that Law? . . . A capacity of knowing that Law. Which is supposed by that Law, at the age of one and twenty years, and in some cases sooner. If this *made* the Father *free*, it shall *make* the Son *free* too. Till then we see the Law allows the Son to have no Will, but he is to be guided by the Will of his Father . . . , who is to understand for him. . . . But after that, the Father and Son are equally *free* . . . whether they be only in the State and under the Law of

Nature, or under the positive Laws of an Establish'd Government. (*Second Treatise*, sec. 59)

One reason that common sense dictates the age of presumed reason is that for Locke reason is itself a fluid rather than static condition. It is not a singular thing thrust upon children in its entirety at some stipulated age. Rather, children develop reason appropriate for their age. Locke articulates this point when he writes:

No Body can think a boy of Three, or Seven Years old, should be argued with, as a grown man. . . . When I say, therefore, that they must be *treated as Rational Creatures*, I mean, that you should make them sensible by the Mildness of your Carriage and the Composure even in your correction of them, that what you do is reasonable in you, and useful and necessary for them. . . . [B]ut it must be by such *Reason* as their Age and Understanding are capable of, and those proposed always *in* very *few and plain Words*. . . . The *Reasons* that moves them must be *obvious*. . . . (*Some Thoughts Concerning Education*, sec. 81–emphasis in the original)

Locke's recognition that reason is developmental is important for understanding how children move into the full state of equality. As previously stated, all children are entitled to be preserved, nourished, and educated by their parents. But these expressions of liberty are conditioned upon children's incapacity rather than their capacity to reason. Since reason is developmental and the basis for entry into a full state of equality, as children grow older and can be presumed to possess more reason they become entitled to a greater variety of liberty independent of their parents and commensurate with the amount of reasoning of other like children of the same age. In effect, then, children gradually move into the state of full equality as they acquire the reason necessary for handling increasingly complex expressions of liberty.

This last point is significant because if children acquire more reason as they grow older, and therefore also a greater variety of liberty, those expressions of liberty enjoyed at a younger age must require less reasoning than those expressions secured later. Therefore, the less reason required for the exercise of a specific liberty, the younger the age at which children can exercise this liberty independent of parental reasoning and judgment. Thus, children are permitted the liberty of crossing the street by themselves before the liberty of driving a car.

Beyond using age as an indicator of reason, this common sense criterion is also relied upon to guarantee that parents cannot use their obligation to educate their children as a way of maintaining lifelong control over them. As discussed earlier, education is one means by which parents bring reason and maturity to their children, thus preparing them for the full state of equality. But Locke sees a problem in this relationship: how to foster and promote parental responsibility for education without making this education a precondition for children moving into a full state of equality. The answer rests in a recognition that this parental responsibility must take place within some fixed yet flexible time period.

By obligating parents to educate their children, Locke, at least implicitly, acknowledges that this process will be lengthy, requiring "an extended period of socialization and learning" during which time their children will develop reasoning capabilities in a manner that fits their "capacity and apprehension" (Richardson 1980, 20). He also recognizes that while parental education of their young is an important means for developing reason, at some point children must be freed from their parents regardless of whether their education was provided or the quality of it. To recognize less than this would be to make achieving the state of reason dependent upon education, thereby granting to parents the absolute ability to deprive their children entrance into a full state of equality either by withholding education from them or providing them with inferior instruction (Tarcov 1984, 73). In effect, if Locke were to condition the ability to know and understand the law of reason, all or in part, on education, this would be tantamount to enslaving children permanently to their parents (*Second Treatise*, secs. 22-24).

To avoid this circumstance, Locke, while he promotes the virtues of education, makes the state of reason dependent upon age alone. In so doing, he implies that aging itself is education and with it comes the ability to reason. Specifically, Locke writes: "Thus we are *born Free*, as we are born Rational; not that we have actually the Exercise of either: Age that brings one, brings with it the other too" (*Second Treatise*, sec. 61; Tarcov 1984, 73). It is worth noting, though, that while he makes this claim, Locke fails to provide any indication as to how this education is to take place in the absence of parental guidance, whether it occurs simply through a child's increasing exposure and experience with the world, or through some other means.

There is an important caveat to the foregoing discussion. Though age alone is generally the condition for majority status and entry into a full state of equality, Locke clearly expresses an understanding that some children, regardless of achieving legal majority, never achieve reason and, therefore, must always remain outside the full state of equality. Locke recognizes that these individuals must always be under the supervision of their parents or guardians. In particular, Locke recognizes that those individuals with severe mental defects, regardless of their biological age, can never reach the full state of equality because they can never fully know the law of reason. Locke writes:

But if through defects that may happen out of the ordinary course of Nature, any one comes not to such a degree of Reason, wherein he might be supposed capable of knowing the Law, and so living within the Rules of it, he is *never capable of being a Free Man*, he is never let loose to the disposure of his own Will (because he knows no bounds to it . . .) but is continued under the Tuition and Government of others, all the time his own Understanding is incapable of that Charge. (*Second Treatise*, sec. 60–emphasis in the original)

Briefly put, Locke is saying, then, that "*Lunatics* and *Idiots* are never set free from the Government of their Parents" (*Second Treatise*, sec. 60–emphasis in the original). Only those children free of mental defects, who reach a designated age of majority or who demonstrate a capacity for liberty-specific reason before the prescribed age for majority can be presumed to know reason and, therefore, can be allowed to enter into a full state of equality.

THE LOCKEAN CHILD AND
THE CONSTITUTION

Children, "merely on account of [their] minority, [are] not beyond the protection of the Constitution" (*Bellotti* v. *Baird* 99 S. Ct. 3035 at 3043. See also *Planned Parenthood of Central Missouri* v. *Danforth* 96 S. Ct. 2831 at 2843). Despite this recognition, though, the Lockean foundation upon which the Constitution rests requires a further recognition that the constitutional liberty of minors be distinguished from those of adults (*Bellotti* v. *Baird* 99 S. Ct. 3035 at 3044). In particular, Lockean-styled liberalism acknowledges that the liberty possessed by minors is less and is protected differently from that liberty enjoyed by adult individuals, such as their parents, who have reached the age of majority. At least three conditions recognized by Lockean-styled liberalism warrant this distinction between the protected liberty of minors and their parents: (1) "the peculiar vulnerability of children; (2) their inability to make critical decisions in an informed, mature manner; (3) and the importance of the parental role in child rearing" (*Bellotti* v. *Baird*, 99 S. Ct. 3035 at 3043). Justice Stevens echoed these Lockean conditions when he wrote:

[Government's] interest in the welfare of its young citizens justifies a variety of protective measures. Because he may not foresee the consequences of his decision, a minor may not make an enforceable bargain. He may not lawfully work or travel where he pleases, or even attend exhibitions of constitutionally protected adult motion pictures. Persons below a certain age may not marry. . . . [Government's] interest in protecting a young person from harm justifies the imposition of restraints on his or her freedom even though comparable restraints on adults would be constitutionally impermissible. (*Planned Parenthood of Central Missouri* v. *Danforth* 96 S. Ct. 2831 at 2856–Justice Stevens, concurring in part and dissenting in part)

Of the three conditions noted above, perhaps the parental role in child rearing is most in keeping with Locke and most important in justifying a lesser constitutional standing for minors. As noted earlier, Lockean-styled liberalism recognizes that ideally it is through their parents that children develop the ability to make critical decisions in an informed and mature manner, thereby losing the peculiar vulnerability that helps to justify the lesser status of their constitutionally protected liberty. This responsibility, upon which all parents are obligated to act, "must be read to include [such things as] the inculcation of moral standards, religious beliefs, and elements of good citizenship" (*Bellotti* v. *Baird* 99 S. Ct. 3035 at 3045 quoting *Wisconsin* v. *Yoder* 92 S. Ct. 1526 at 1542). Indeed, parental instruction is so important to the proper development of children that Lockean-styled liberalism can be understood as recognizing that parents "who have demonstrated sufficient commitment to [their] children [are] thereafter entitled to raise the children from undue state interference" (*Hodgson* v. *Minnesota* 111 L. Ed. 2d 344 at 368).

Though parental instruction of their children generally resides outside of governmental intrusion, Lockean-styled liberalism also recognizes that government, if it so chooses, can take positive action to enhance parents' guidance and direction of their children through the passage of "laws designed to aid the discharge of that responsibility" (*Hodgson* v. *Minnesota* 111 L. Ed. 2d 244 at 369 quoting *Ginsberg* v. *New York* 390 U.S. 629 at 639) so long as these laws do not substitute government authority for the parental authority they are trying to promote. Such actions may be based upon the prudent determination that parental authority is basic to the structure and continuation of the political or civic community. This is because when parents properly execute their authority, they bring their children to maturity and reason, thereby enabling them to enter into the community fully aware of the obligations associated with such membership (*H.L.* v. *Matheson* 67 L. Ed. 2d 288 at 399).

Thus, with its Lockean-styled foundation, the Constitution, too, must be interpreted as recognizing a narrower range of liberty for dependent minors and allowing for a lesser degree of protection for this liberty in order to guard dependent minors from their own immaturity and lack of reasoning (Stern 1985, 881). In so doing, the Constitution sets forth a general rule that minors generally can "exercise the rights they do have only through and with parental consent" (*Hodgson* v. *Minnesota* 111 L. Ed.

2d 344 at 391–Justice Kennedy concurring in part and dissenting in part). By placing these restrictions on the liberty of minors, Lockean-styled liberalism and the Constitution acknowledge that

> the tradition of parental authority is not inconsistent with [the] tradition of individual liberty; rather, the former is one of the basic presuppositions of the latter. Legal restrictions on minors, especially those supportive of the parental role, may be important to the child's chances for growth and maturity that make eventual participation in a free society meaningful and rewarding. (*Bellotti* v. *Baird* 99 S. Ct 3035 at 3045-3046)

But in recognizing the important role of parental authority to the development of minors and government's choice to promote and encourage the former, the Lockean interpretation of the Constitution means that this document must also be understood as acknowledging that parents have an obligation to exercise their authority in a manner that is not absolute, harmful to their children, or discourages the development of reason. Thus, the Constitution properly interpreted recognizes that a principal liberty possessed by children is the "right to develop the capacity to think maturely and independently" of their parents and that this liberty in turn limits the power of parents "to dictate their children's conduct and beliefs throughout minority" (Stern 1985, 873). Therefore, as the Supreme Court has noted:

> parents may be free to become martyrs themselves. But it does not follow that they are free, in identical circumstances, to make martyrs of their children before they have reached the age of full and legal discretion when they can make that choice themselves." (*Prince* v. *Massachusetts* 321 U.S. 158 at 174)

Accordingly, government's responsibility to protect children from abuse of parental authority or neglect of parental obligations grows from this recognition. Indeed, it is constitutionally incumbent upon government to guarantee that minors lacking the competence to protect themselves from the excesses and abuses of parental authority be so protected. Thus, government must intervene in the parent-child relationship on behalf of children in those instances where the exercise of parental authority has implications for the three areas of liberty—preservation, education, and nourishment—children possess under Lockean-styled liberalism. For Lockean-based government to do less would be to ignore the fundamental purpose for which it is formed: to secure liberty.

In addition, government may find it necessary to provide children with the opportunity to develop the reasoning abilities necessary for freeing themselves from parental direction and control. One way in which this can be done is for government to adopt Locke's reliance upon a legally defined age as "a rough but fair approximation of maturity and judgment" and the principal criterion for ascending to full equality and liberty (*Hodgson* v. *Minnesota* 111 L. Ed. 2d 344 at 392–Justice Kennedy concurring in part and dissenting in part). But in keeping with the Lockean-styled recognition that different ages of presumed reason exist for different expressions of liberty, government also would need to approach the use of an age criterion with some flexibility.

MINOR WOMEN AND THE ABORTION DECISION

A minor woman experiencing an unwanted pregnancy is faced with a paradox. Physically and biologically, she is mature enough to give birth. Yet in many life choices her age is likely to "subject her to a statutory presumption of immaturity" (Buchanan 1982, 554-555). Though she is physically mature enough to give birth to a child, she may be too young legally to vote, drive a car, or even attend certain motion pictures being shown at local theaters. The reason: the legal presumption of immaturity accompanies all of these laws.

This juxtaposition of physical maturity and legally presumed immaturity is one of the primary problems surrounding teenage pregnancies and their resolution (Buchanan 1982, 555). But the immediacy of pregnancy coupled with the dramatic changes childbirth and parenting bring to a minor woman's life further complicate any resolution. These natural realities of unwanted pregnancy make any liberty interest she has in determining how to resolve such a pregnancy unique from other liberty interests to which she might make a claim. Justice Lewis Powell clearly recognizes these unique circumstances when he wrote:

> The pregnant minor's options are much different from those facing a minor in other situations, such as deciding whether to marry. A minor not permitted to marry before the age of majority is required to simply postpone her decision. She and her intended spouse may preserve the opportunity for later marriage should they continue to desire it. A pregnant adolescent, however, cannot preserve for long the possibility of aborting, which effectively expires in a matter of weeks from the onset of the pregnancy. . . . In addition, the fact of having a child brings with it adult legal responsibility, for parenthood, like the attainment of the age of majority, is one of the traditional criteria for the termination of the legal disabilities of minority. In sum, there are few situations in which denying a minor the right to make an important decision will have consequences so grave and indelible. (*Bellotti* v. *Baird* 99 S. Ct. 3035 at 3048)

Acknowledging the paradox of physiological maturity and legally presumed immaturity compounded by the unique circumstances of unwanted pregnancies, one must wonder how then is a minor woman's liberty interest in the abortion decision to be understood? As noted earlier in this chapter, Lockean-styled liberalism recognizes that a principal criterion for individuals possessing liberty is their knowing reason. Reason, in turn, is roughly measured by children attaining a particular age at which the former can be presumed to exist. It is this presumption of reason that distinguishes liberty-bearing individuals of majority (adults) from nonliberty-bearing individuals of minority (children).

In addition, Lockean-styled liberalism recognizes that some expressions of liberty require less fully developed reason while other expressions require reason to be more fully developed. Therefore, there is not a single age upon which minors enter majority and the full state of liberty. Instead, minors increase the range of expressions of liberty they may exercise independently of their parents as they grow older and can be presumed to possess more reason. Whether minors are, then, otherwise entitled to a particular expression of liberty rests on a determination of the degree of reason necessary for exercising it and the approximate age at which minors can be presumed to possess this reason. When minors reach this age, they must be presumed to possess sufficient reason to exercise that expression of liberty independent of parental consent. From that age onward for that expression of liberty, they have obtained majority, and government must protect them in its exercise.

On the other hand, minors who have not reached the age of presumed reason in regard to a particular expression of liberty must be presumed to lack sufficient reason to exercise it. They must be judged incompetent. They remain under the authority of their parents who must reason and judge for them. Government's task here is to respect and not interfere with parental guidance and instruction in these matters unless the parents act in ways harmful or threatening to the preservation of their children, or in other ways to suggest the forfeiture of their parental authority over their offspring. To do more than this violates the Lockean distinction between the public and private sphere of human existence. It does so by substituting government's reason and judgment for that of the parents in matters far removed from government's legitimate purpose.

When one applies these criteria, then, the extent and nature of minor teenage women's access to a liberty interest in the abortion decision independent of their parents require a determination of both the extent of reason necessary to exercise this liberty and the age at which these minor women can be presumed to possess this reason. Regarding the first determination, it is essential to recognize that unwanted pregnancies present minor women with three distinct choices: giving birth and assuming parental responsibility for the child, giving birth but placing the child for adoption, or having an abortion. The extent of reason necessary for determining the appropriateness of these choices to the resolution of an unwanted pregnancy is generally similar but some differences do exist. Take, for instance, the extent of reason necessary in either choosing to have an abortion or giving birth and assuming parental responsibility for the child. A woman considering the abortion or birth options needs to be able to make a reasoned judgment about the medical effects (both physical and psychological) of both alternatives. Thus, both alternatives require a woman to be capable of making a reasoned medical judgment. But here the similarities between the two alternatives end.

Consideration of the birth and parenthood alternative requires a pregnant woman to make reasoned considerations beyond the medical judgment noted above. She also must be able to make reasoned judgments about her ability to perform the Lockean responsibilities and obligations associated with parenting that will be legally and morally thrust upon her when her child is born. Specifically, she must reason whether she is able or will be able to secure for her child the liberty to which all children are entitled, that being education, nourishment, and preservation.

A minor woman must additionally be aware of the added burden her age brings to her ability to fulfill her parental responsibilities and obligations. For example, in considering the birth and parenthood option, minor women must be cognitive of the likelihood that given their "probable education, employment skills, financial resources . . . motherhood may be exceptionally burdensome" for them and their children (*Ohio* v. *Akron Reproductive Health Center* 111 L. Ed. 2d 405 at 428). Given the probability of this condition existing, pregnant teenage women considering motherhood must ask themselves if they will be capable of nourishing and preserving their children or if they will have to either temporarily or permanently forfeit those responsibilities to other individuals.

Minor teenage women also must consider the implication for the children that they would bear, that they themselves lack reason and are still dependent upon their own parents for it. Such a condition is important because from a Lockean understanding of parental obligation, it is the responsibility of the parents or some other individual of majority to reason for the children, particularly during infancy and youth. Therefore, individuals who do not yet sufficiently know reason themselves cannot reason for others. This is the predicament that all women of minority confronting unwanted pregnancies experience. To choose the birth and parenting option requires them to have sufficient reason to know that they initially lack the reason to reason for their infant children. It requires minor women to recognize the probable need to at least temporarily forfeit their parental responsibility for their children to some other individual of majority until that time that they themselves are capable of carrying out this responsibility.

Given the extra dimension of reason required of the birth and parenthood option, this alternative actually requires a greater extent of reasoning from a teenage woman experiencing an unwanted pregnancy than does the abortion decision. Minor women contemplating the abortion decision need only to possess sufficient reasoning skills to address the medical judgment that has to be made. On the other hand, pregnant teenage women considering the birth and parenthood alternative must possess sufficient reasoning to make the medical judgment in addition to judgments concerning their ability to perform the parental obligation required by Lockean-styled liberalism. Thus, contrary to popular belief as expressed in current parental consent laws, there actually appears to be at least an equal, if not greater, justification for parental involvement and consent in the birth and parenthood option.

Given the extent of reasoning required in the abortion decision, at what age can minor women be presumed to possess the reason necessary for independently making this decision? Developmental psychology may be helpful in answering that question. Developmental psychologists divide adolescence into three approximate stages. Early adolescence is generally considered to commence from ages twelve to thirteen. Middle adolescence is fourteen and fifteen years old, and late adolescence begins at approximately sixteen years of age. Formal reasoning abilities generally begin to emerge during early adolescence and continue to develop throughout the adolescent years (Rodman et al. 1984, 82).

By middle adolescence, developmental research suggests that teenagers generally possess sufficient reason to select alternative medical treatment with full understanding of their risks and benefits (Grisso and Vierling 1978; O'Keeffe and Jones 1990; Weithorn and Campbell 1982). At this age, the "logical reasoning, in which various alternatives can be evaluated, is potentially available" (Rodman et al. 1984, 133-144). Since middle adolescence covers minors ranging from fourteen to fifteen years of age, prudence suggests that the latter stage of middle adolescence — fifteen years of age, be selected as the age at which otherwise minor women can be presumed to possess the reason necessary to exercise a liberty interest in the abortion decision independent of parental consent. Adjusting the age to the higher end of middle adolescence increases the likelihood that the potential for logical reasoning will actually be a reality while keeping the presumption of reason within the developmental stage in which this reason first appears. It is important to note, though, that this designated age of presumed reason is not etched in stone. As developmental psychologists refine their understanding, this age can be raised or lowered accordingly. But until this occurs, it is both reasonable and prudent to accept current knowledge as the point at which minor teenage women can be presumed to possess the reason necessary to make the abortion decision independent of any need for parental consent.

Thus, at late middle adolescence, if minor women are presumed to have obtained "sufficient maturity to make a fully informed decision, [they are] then entitled to make [their] abortion decision independently." It further means that government "cannot constitutionally permit . . . disregard of the abortion decision of [minor women] who [have] been determined to be mature and fully competent to assess the implications of the choice[s they have] made" (*Bellotti* v. *Baird* 99 S. Ct. 3035 at 3052). Rather, government is obligated to protect this expression of liberty.

However, contemporary abortion statutes requiring parental consent do not apply this Lockean-styled standard. Instead, these laws make no distinction between minor women who have reached the age of presumed reason and those who have not. To the contrary, these laws treat all minor women as if they lack sufficient reason to make an informed and independent decision about abortion. Building on this presumption, contemporary parental consent laws force minor women who have reached the age of presumed reason to use a judicial bypass process to convince judges that they do indeed possess the reason necessary to make an abortion decision independent of parental consent.

In so doing, rather than protecting the liberty interest these minors have in the abortion decision, government hinders it and exposes it to the arbitrary whims of judges who either refuse to perform their official duties or use their official positions to impose their private morality upon these mature minors. For example, in Minnesota some judges simply refuse to hear judicial bypass petitions, thereby forcing minor women to travel as far as 250 miles to find a judge willing to hear their petitions (O'Keeffe and Jones 1990, 78). When minor women find judges who will hear their bypass petitions, the judges' own values on the morality of abortion are likely to unduly influence their decisions regarding these minor women's requests. For example, a month after the Michigan state legislature enacted its parental consent legislation, a state judge commented that "only in cases of incest or rape of a white girl by a black man" would he offer a waiver for an abortion (Wilerson 1991, A19).

Judicial bypass procedures further hinder the liberty interest in the abortion decision of minor women who have reached the age of presumed reason by requiring these minors to also possess sufficient reason to know how to maneuver themselves through a maze of judicial procedures, paperwork, and bureaucracy. Take, for instance, Justice Blackmun's characterization of the Ohio judicial bypass procedure under review in *Ohio* v. *Akron Reproductive Health Center*:

> The obstacle course begins when the minor first enters the courthouse to fill out the complaint form. The "pleading trap" . . . requires the minor to choose between three forms. The first alleges *only* maturity; the second *only* . . . best interest. . . . Only if the minor chooses the third form, which alleges both, . . . may the minor attempt to prove both maturity *and* best interest. . . . (111 L. Ed. 2d 405 at 429–Justice Blackmun dissenting; emphasis in the original)

As the above discussion indicates, minor women who have reached the age of presumed reason regarding the abortion decision enjoy the same liberty interest in this decision as women of majority. Parental consent is not required and government responsibility is to protect, not to encumber this liberty interest. In contrast, minor women below the age of presumed reason cannot make an independent decision about abortion. For these minor women, parental consent is still a prerequisite before they can undergo an abortion (see *Second Treatise*, sec. 61; *Hodgson* v. *Minnesota* 111 L. Ed. 2d 344 at 391). Their parents, therefore, still need to reason for them. In exercising this judgment, parents have great leeway in instructing and directing their daughters' decision as to what course of action in resolving their unwanted pregnancies is in their best interest. This conclusion includes all possible alternatives to unwanted pregnancies: birth and parenting, birth and adoption, and abortion.

Admittedly, this requirement of parental consent for all minor women who are under the age of reason may not always result in what others consider to be in these minor women's best interest. Indeed, a great deal of debate occurs over the Lockean directive to parents "to take care of their offspring . . . to inform [her] mind . . . and govern [her] actions . . . till reason takes its place" (*Second Treatise*, sec. 58). For example, addressing this particular point as it relates specifically to parental opposition to abortion, a New York State Family Court Judge wrote:

> In my observations, mothers who have opposed their unmarried daughters' efforts to secure abortions variously have expressed a vengeful desire to punish the daughter for sexual activity by making her suffer the unwanted child, a fervor to impose a religious conviction the mother has failed to instill in her daughter, a hope of caring for her daughter's baby as her own because of an inability . . . to bear another child herself . . . , a defensive or resentful attitude because *she* bore illegitimate children without . . . being able to secure an abortion, or a general distaste for abortion. (Dembitz 1980, 1255)

Despite these questionable motives for opposing their daughters' abortions, Lockean-styled liberalism does not expect parents, any more than other individuals, to possess or exercise perfect reason. They need only to know it as "well as . . . others . . . who live . . . under the Law" and who apply it in ways to help, instruct, and preserve their children (*Second Treatise*, sec. 170). Thus, except for certain severe situations that will be discussed shortly, what others deem faulty reason resulting in less than the best interest of their minor daughters being promoted, does not result in parents forfeiting their authority over their minor daughters. Accordingly, there is little or no justification for "best interest" intervention by government on behalf of minor women beneath the age of presumed reason.

Thus, current parental consent laws with judicial bypass procedures allowing minor women under the age of presumed reason to nevertheless petition the courts for a ruling that their parents' denial of consent is not in their best interest, lacks Lockean justification. Judicial bypass procedures permit the courts' definition of best interest to be substituted for the parents. They substitute the reason and judgment of government for that of the parents. In so doing, judicial bypass procedures ignore the Lockean recognition of the primacy of parents' authority over their children that is normally given great leeway. By ignoring this recognition, contemporary judicial bypass procedures intrude too deeply into the parent-child relationship, thereby putting aside the Lockean distinction between the public and private sphere of human existence. If the opposite of these arguments were true and the judicial bypass processes found in current parental consent laws were valid, the courts could make the "private realm of family life conform to some [judicial] designed ideal" (*Hodgson* v. *Minnesota* 111 L. Ed. 2d 544 at 372). And this likely would be done by judges whose decisions "must necessarily reflect personal and societal values and mores" but nevertheless conflict and oppose the private reasoning some parents are trying to foster in their children (*Bellotti* v. *Baird* 99 S. Ct. 3035 at 3054). If the best interest argument is valid here, then government-imposed conformity could extend not just to abortion but to *any* area of family life government chooses to standardize.

Admittedly, requiring parental consent for those minor women under the age of presumed reason and denying them the opportunity to petition the court for a reversal of their parents' denial of consent is likely to encourage these minors to circumvent this consent requirement or to delay obtaining it. Indeed, available empirical evidence suggests that this is the case. For example, the parental consent law in Massachusetts has forced nearly one-third of that state's minor women seeking abortions to travel to neighboring states where parental consent or notification is not required. Parental consent laws also stymie effective and timely parental involvement in the abortion decision. For example, current parental consent and notification laws result in abortions occurring later in the pregnancy of minor women than for women of majority. Twenty-three percent of all abortions performed on minor women under the age of 15 take place during the second trimester, whereas for women 20 to 24 years of age the figure is only 8 percent (O'Keeffe and Jones 1990, 78). After Minnesota's parental notification statute went into effect, the proportion of second trimester abortions among minor women in that state increased by 18 percent (Donovan 1992, 21). Finally, parental consent laws contribute to "children having children." Since the introduction of Minnesota's parental notification law, the birthrate for minors affected by the law (those under 17 years of age) has registered a dramatic increase of 38 percent as compared with only a .3 percent increase among 18- and 19-year-old women not covered by the law (O'Keeffe and Jones 1990, 78).

Nevertheless, these facts do not undermine the Lockean-based legitimacy of parental consent as much as they address the current failure of government to adequately promote a proper understanding of the need for this consent. For parental consent to work, government must foster its importance and use. Under the Lockean-styled perspective developed in this and preceding chapters, government needs only to be morally tolerant. It does not have to be morally indifferent. Thus, government is free to take a moral position on abortion in accordance to the Lockean-styled limitations specified in this and earlier chapters. In so doing, government is free to recognize and promote the value of the parental involvement in the procreative decisions minor women beneath the age of presumed reason are likely to face. Indeed, there is little doubt that government

> furthers a constitutionally permissible end when by encouraging an unmarried pregnant minor to seek the help and advice of her parents in making the very important decision whether or not to bear a child. That is a grave decision, and a girl of tender years, under emotional stress, may be ill-equipped to make it without mature advice and emotional support. (*Planned Parenthood of Central Missouri* v. *Danforth* 96 S. Ct. 2831 at 2851-Justice Stewart concurring)

However, if government chooses to promote and encourage parental involvement in the procreative decisions of minor women under the age of presumed reason, it *should* be sensitive to the need to foster this involvement across all procreative decisions concerning unwanted pregnancies that these minors are likely to confront, not just abortion. Currently, this is not the case. Conventional government policies concerning the procreative decisions of immature minors place greatest emphasis on promoting parental involvement in the abortion decision rather than on other procreative decisions. As one leading commentator writes:

A majority of the states have laws that authorize a pregnant teenager to consent to prenatal care and labor and delivery services, and no state requires a minor to have parental consent to continue a pregnancy to term. Once a teenager has borne a child, she can decide whether to raise the child herself or put it up for adoption. Yet in more than one-third of the states, unless she first consults her parents . . . a young woman cannot decide on her own that it would be best not to have a child and then seek medical care to terminate a pregnancy. (Donovan 1992, 17)

This inconsistency exists despite the widely accepted medical understanding that pregnancy for women of all ages produces greater health risks than abortion does, thereby presenting a greater threat to a woman's self-preservation. For example, "women giving birth are 100 times more likely than women having abortion to need major abdominal surgery for complications, and they are 11 times more likely to die" (Donovan 1992, 20). In addition, the inconsistency in regulating teenage birth and abortion ignores the greater extent of reason needed in choosing the former over the latter.

Though the above discussion underscores the necessity of parental consent for all minor women under the age of presumed reason, this consent is not absolute or completely outside the scope of government action. As noted earlier in this chapter, Lockean-styled liberalism recognizes that all children possess a liberty interest in preservation that limits parental authority from exercising life or death over them. In addition, Lockean-styled liberalism also recognizes that, if improperly applied in ways harmful to their children, parents may forfeit their authority over their children and have it transferred to another. Take, for instance, situations in which minor women presumed not to have sufficient reason to independently make the abortion decision are confronted by life-threatening pregnancies. Such pregnancies are a direct challenge to these minor women's liberty interest in preservation. Therefore, their parents have no choice but to secure the preservation of their minor daughters by having these pregnancies aborted. In these situations, the parents have no other choice. As noted previously in this chapter, nature's law commands parents to preserve their children, and nothing can absolve them of this responsibility (*Second Treatise*, sec. 63, 170).

Indeed, parents who would insist that their minor daughters continue with life-threatening pregnancies would have to be judged as forfeiting their responsibility and authority over these children. In these instances, the consent of a single parent would be sufficient. Without this, government must assume this responsibility and use its coercive authority against those parents in order to secure the preservation of these minor women. For government to do less than this would make these minor women susceptible to the absolute authority of their parents over them, an authority in this case literally being exercised to decide their life or death.

This same limit on parental consent and the recognition of government responsibility extends to situations in which minor women who cannot be presumed to possess the reason to make an independent decision become pregnant from incest rape. Fathers who commit such acts of violence against their own daughters clearly forfeit any authority over how the daughter resolve these unwanted pregnancies. In these instances, the mothers' consent is sufficient. Failing this, government must assume the responsibility for these minor women's well-being, either directly or transferring the forfeited parental authority to foster parents or other guardians.

CONCLUSION

The Lockean-styled framework developed in this chapter sets forth a simple and direct approach regarding minor women and the liberty interest in abortion. Briefly reiterated, this perspective distinguishes between minor women who have reached the age at which they can be presumed to have sufficient reason to make the abortion decision independent of parental consent and those minor women toward whom this presumption cannot be made. Those minor women who have reached the age of presumed reason are entitled to a liberty interest in the abortion decision equal to that of women of majority. Neither their parents nor government possesses any legitimate authority to prevent their exercise of this liberty.

The reverse is true for minor women who have not reached the age of presumed reason. Lacking the presumption of reason, these minor women need parental consent, and government can require it. The abortions of unwanted pregnancies resulting from life-threatening pregnancies and incest rape are the exception to this general rule. The first represents a threat to these minor women's liberty interest in preservation. The second represents the forfeiture of parental authority. In both instances, government has a responsibility to guarantee the best interests of these minor women. Other exceptions to the general rule governing parental consent for minor women under the age of presumed reason may exist. The case of non-incest rape is one. But these exceptions are based upon the prudent consideration of government and are recognized by statutory law. They represent an expansion of those required forms of protection arising from Lockean-styled liberalism.

Admittedly, not all minors who reach the age of presumed reason actually possess the reason to make the abortion decision without parental consent. Nor will all minor women under this age lack that reason. Nevertheless, the Lockean-styled perspective formulated in this chapter ensures that the vast majority of minor women both at and under the presumed age of reason are extended the degree of independence in the abortion decision they should have.

6

Fetal-Being Personhood, Preservation and Limits on the Abortion Decision

Adult and mature minor women enjoy a liberty interest in the abortion decision that government is prohibited from abridging or infringing. But under Locke's liberalism, this liberty interest in the abortion decision, like all liberty, "has a Law of Nature to govern [and limit] it, which obligates everyone" equally (*Second Treatise*, sec. 6). Thus, a liberty interest in the abortion decision is not the same as a license to make or act on that decision as a woman absolutely wishes to do. Like all liberty, it is limited first by nature's mandate that individuals are not to "quit [their] Station [in life] willfully (*Second Treatise*, sec. 6). Accordingly, individuals are not to exercise their liberty in ways likely to threaten their preservation. In regard to abortion, this limit means that a woman cannot actualize her liberty interest in the abortion decision in ways harmful to herself or that is likely to threaten her preservation. This limit, coupled with its corollary that individuals should "preserve the rest of [person]kind" when their own preservation is not at risk (*Second Treatise*, sec. 6), is also the foundation and justification for government regulation of abortion methods and procedures.

The recognition and acceptance of this limit point out an aspect of the conventional pro-choice position that is fundamentally flawed when applied to the constitutional understanding of liberty. A popular pro-choice pronouncement is that a woman has a right to absolute control over her body. But in a political community premised upon Lockean-styled liberalism, this position cannot be the foundation for a liberty interest in abortion. If a woman had the complete bodily autonomy attributed to her by conventional pro-choice thinking, she would be able to alienate her self-preservation, the most fundamental of the inalienable rights recognized by Locke's interpretation of nature's law. She would have the license to kill herself or enslave herself (Glenn 1975, 75). But Locke's law of nature prohibits these actions.

Nature's law further limits liberty through a second mandate stipulating that "no one ought to harm another in his Life, Health, Liberty, or Possession" (*Second Treatise*, sec. 6). In short, individuals are not to use their liberty in ways harmful to themselves or others. This second limit has an impact on a woman's liberty interest in the abortion decision by drawing attention to the effect the exercise of this liberty has on the developing life of the fetal-being. It underscores the fact that a woman's exercise of her liberty interest in the abortion decision and a fetal-being's developing life cannot be severed and are in conflict. Simply put, the inseparability and conflict between abortion and the fetal-being's life come down to the realization that for a woman to exercise her liberty interest in abortion, she has no choice but to destroy the developing fetal-being and its potential for meaningful human life. Stressing these points, one commentator observes:

> "At the moment of conception, there is created a potentiality for life. As the pregnancy progresses, the potentiality becomes greater. Any decision to terminate the pregnancy once effectuated by action cuts off the potentiality. Once the fetus is aborted, any possibility of life is lost forever." (Fuqua 1980, 287-288)

But this second limit really can restrict a woman's liberty interest in the abortion decision only if, at some point in its development, the fetal-being acquires the legal status of personhood. As discussed more fully later in this chapter, Locke's liberalism suggests a point before birth at which the fetal-being acquires personhood and, therefore, secures its preservation through government's application of the second limit against a woman's liberty interest in the abortion decision. That point is the stage in fetal development at which the fetal-being possesses both physiological viability and humanness, thereby approximating the Lockean-born child with the capability to learn reason.

The combination of this second limit and the recognition of the fetal-being's personhood have an impact on a woman's liberty interest in the abortion decision by establishing its outer boundaries. At the point at which the fetal-being achieves personhood, nature's law against individuals exercising their liberty in ways harmful to other persons makes the fetal-being's liberty in preservation superior to a woman's liberty interest in the abortion decision, except under those circumstances in which an abortion is imperative to securing the health and preservation of the woman. At the point of the fetal-being attaining personhood and acting on its original and only reason for existence—i.e., to secure liberty, government is obligated to secure the physiological and brain-viable fetal-being's preservation. This is done by prohibiting all post-viability abortions except when the life of the mother is in jeopardy or her health is seriously at risk, and regulating and prescribing abortion procedures of post-viability fetal-beings to promote their preservation when they must be aborted in order to maintain a woman's health and preservation.

Thus, nature's law limiting liberty combined with the Lockean conditions for personhood mean that a woman's liberty interest in the abortion decision is "a limited . . . right to determine whether to terminate a pregnancy" (*Webster* v. *Reproductive Health Services* 106 L. Ed. 2d 410 at 460–Justice Blackmun dissenting). It "must be considered against important [government] interest" in regulating the liberty interest in abortion to guarantee the preservation of both the women undergoing abortions and the viable fetal-beings who have sufficiently developed to have the status of personhood bestowed upon them (*Roe* v. *Wade* 93 S. Ct. 705 at 727). The remainder of Chapter 6 more thoroughly discusses these limits and their actual impact on a woman's liberty interest in abortion.

RESTRICTING ABORTION TO GUARANTEE SELF-PRESERVATION

When government acts to protect individuals against the excessive exercise of liberty and potential harmful consequences resulting from such actions, it acts in ways consistent with nature's commands of self-preservation and the preservation of others. Thus, Lockean government passes and enforces such laws as those against suicide and the illegal sale and use of narcotics. The same Lockean understanding of nature's law justifying government regulation of these excesses in liberty justifies its regulation of medical procedures, such as abortion, that are likely to bring harm to individuals and threaten their self-preservation.

Deaths from legal abortion are actually quite rare. In countries where abortion is legal and relatively accessible, deaths from abortion average less than one per 100,000 abortions (Costa 1991, 97). In 1985, abortion mortality in the United States was .4 deaths per 100,000 abortions. Of the 1.6 million abortions performed that year, only six women are known to have died after undergoing legal abortion (Gold 1990, 28).

Though the likelihood of death from legal abortion is rare, the fact that some women do die underscores that abortion, like any other medical surgical procedure, still places patients at some risk. Several factors contribute to the risk women face when they undergo abortion. The time of gestation at which the abortion occurs, the method of abortion, and the type of anesthesia used all affect abortion mortality (Gold 1990, 29-30). Of these factors, the type of anesthesia accounts for most abortion-related deaths, with general anesthesia riskier than local anesthesia (Costa 1991, 98). But contrary to what popular abortion restrictions suggest, the type of facilities in which abortion takes place does not contribute to abortion mortality. For all but the latest and most dangerous abortions, clinics are as safe as hospitals (Gold 1990, 30-32).

That some deaths do occur, or are likely to occur, justifies government exercise of its Lockean obligation to foster individual self-preservation. The Supreme Court has recognized this Lockean obligation in *Roe* v. *Wade*. Justice Blackmun, speaking for the Court's majority, wrote that government "has a legitimate interest in seeing to it that abortion, like any other medical procedure, is performed under circumstances that insure maximum safety for the patient" (93 S. Ct. 705 at 725). Continuing, he notes that this government interest in the self-preservation of women undergoing abortion "extends at least to the attending physicians and their staffs, the facilities carrying out the abortion, [and] to the availability of care after the abortion is completed" (93 S. Ct. 705 at 725). It seems logical to add to this list the safety of the abortion procedure used because government in its effort to promote the self-preservation of women undergoing abortion should be able to require the attending physician to use the safest procedure available for the gestation time at which the abortion is to take place.

By regulating the safety of the abortion process, government is not limitless in the kinds of regulations and control that it can impose. To the contrary, the Lockean expectation of moral tolerance means that government is "not free, under the guise of protecting maternal health . . . , to intimidate women into continuing their pregnancies" (*Thornburgh* v. *American College of Obstetricians and Gynecologists* 90 L. Ed. 2d 779 at 793; see also *Planned Parenthood of Central Missouri* v. *Danforth*, 96 S. Ct. 2831 at 2845). Rather, government's interest in regulating the abortion process must be the self-preservation of the women undergoing abortion. Thus, government cannot regulate the abortion process in ways that "depart from acceptable medical practice" (*Akron* v. *Akron Center for Reproductive Health* 76 L. Ed. 2d 687 at 703; see also *Simopoulos* v. *Virginia* 76 L. Ed. 2d. 755 at 763).

For example, in regard to the Lockean expectation of moral tolerance, government under the guise of protecting maternal health and preservation cannot pursue an anti-abortion morality and seek to impose it upon women by requiring abortions to take place in more costly hospitals rather than in less expensive abortion clinics when there is no medically proven reason for doing so. These location restrictions coerce moral behavior rather than merely influence it. In so doing, they violate the Lockean dictate of moral tolerance. In *Akron* v. *Akron Center for Reproductive Health*, the Supreme Court implicitly acknowledged this Lockean requirement by ruling that location restrictions on abortion that seek to discourage and reduce the incidence of abortion by increasing its cost are constitutionally impermissible (76 L. Ed. 2d 687 at 706).

In addition, government cannot prohibit a specific popular and widely used method of abortion in an effort to discourage and reduce the incidence of abortion when that method is the safest and most effective one available. To do so would force "a woman and her physician to terminate her pregnancy by methods more dangerous to her health [and self-preservation] than the method outlawed" (*Planned Parenthood of Central Missouri* v. *Danforth* 96 S. Ct. 2831 at 2845). On the other hand, government would be acting on behalf of a woman's self-preservation if, based upon accepted medical knowledge and practice, it required abortion providers to use the medically recognized safest method of abortion available for the fetal-being's gestation, except when the abortion provider concludes that for a particular patient another method is safer and therefore preferable. Thus, for second trimester abortions of nonviable fetal-beings, government could reasonably require that these abortions be carried out through the safer method of dilatation and evacuation rather than the more risky amnioinfusion with a saline solution (Costa 1991, 111-112).

Following this line of analysis, it is reasonable to conclude from a Lockean perspective that government also could prescribe and justify the use of RU 486 as the preferred and safest method for early abortions. RU 486, also known as the abortion pill, provides for abortions that are cheaper and more private, and that can be performed sooner than other early abortion methods (Boland 1990, 410). When taken under medical supervision, RU 486 produces few serious side effects, the most common being regular bleeding, such as during a heavy menstrual period. Unlike other early abortion methods, RU 486 has the advantage of not requiring any anesthesia—the leading cause of abortion mortality—or instrument interventions that can cause cervical injury or uterine perforation (Costa 1991, 114).

In prescribing RU 486 for abortion during the first eight weeks of pregnancy, government would be acting in its Lockean interest in a woman's health and preservation by also establishing regulations for its use based upon the current state of medical knowledge about the drug. Indeed, model statutes for regulating the use of RU 486 have been proposed. For example, one commentator proposes a model statute wherein:

[T]he physician shall first determine if the unborn [fetal-being] is more than the eight weeks gestation age by using the degree of care, skill, and proficiency commonly exercised by the . . . prudent physician. . . .

1. No abortion using RU 486 shall be performed after the eighth week of pregnancy. 2. RU 486, when administered to terminate a pregnancy within the first eight weeks of pregnancy, shall be administered by a licensed doctor or nurse . . . and only in a licensed clinic or hospital. (Hass 1990, 295)

In requiring that RU 486 be taken under strict medical supervision, it would also seem reasonable that government could define, within current medical practices and knowledge, what that supervision entails. One such model regarding this supervision comes from the French experience with the drug. Three physician visits are required, and a fourth is strongly recommended. The first visit is for pregnancy testing, counseling, and signing a consent form. On the second visit, an oral dose of RU 486 is delivered. On the third visit, a prostaglandin is administered; this increases the success of the abortion and speeds it along. The fourth visit is to guarantee that the abortion was complete and to check for any serious side effects (Costa 1991, 114).

THE ABORTION DECISION AND FETAL-BEING PERSONHOOD

A woman's liberty interest in the abortion decision is limited further by nature's law against individuals exercising their liberty in ways harmful to other persons. But for this limit to restrict a woman's liberty interest in the abortion decision, at some point after conception but before birth the fetal-being must acquire the legal status of personhood. At this point of legally recognized personhood, the fetal-being ceases being a potential person and becomes an actual person with a liberty interest in preservation that must command the moral respect of others (Rubenfeld 1991, 621). As it is required to do for all other individuals, government is obligated to guarantee that the fetal-being receives this moral respect from other individuals and that its preservation is secured. This is accomplished by government applying its coercive power to proscribe all abortions after the point at which the fetal-being acquires personhood—all abortions except those necessitated by women experiencing health- or life-threatening pregnancies. But from a Lockean perspective, when does a fetal-being acquire personhood and a liberty interest in preservation? Briefly revisiting earlier discussions can shed some light on this question.

First, a Lockean individual residing in a state of full and equal liberty is a born person of majority who can be presumed to possess the reason necessary for knowing and understanding nature's law. Absent any evidence to the contrary, the Constitution, as a Lockean-styled attempt to protect and secure liberty, must also be recognized as extending the full and equal state of liberty to only born persons of majority who possess the reason to know and understand nature's law and how that law manifests itself in the civil community. Admittedly, this Lockean understanding has never been fully evident in constitutional interpretation. But on occasion, the Supreme Court has expressed this view, at least in part. For example, in *Roe* v. *Wade* (93 S. Ct. 705 at 728-29), Justice Blackmun writing for the Court's majority explicitly stated that in all instances in which the Constitution uses the word "person," "the use of the word is such that it has application only postnatally. None [of the usage of the word person] indicates, with any assurance, that it has any pre-natal application" (93 S. Ct. 705 at 729). Echoing this sentiment, legal theorist Ronald Dworkin writes:

> The principle that the fetus is not a constitutional person fits better with other parts of our law. . . . The best historical evidence shows . . . that even anti-abortion laws . . . were adopted to protect the health of the mother and the privileges of the medical profession, not out of any recognition of a fetus's rights. . . . So the better interpretation of our constitutional law holds that a fetus is not a constitutional person. (Dworkin 1989, 50)

Defining individuals enjoying the full and equal state of liberty to include only those born persons of majority who can be presumed to possess reason generally excludes children (persons of minority) from this state. As discussed in Chapter 5, Locke recognizes that since children do not possess the reason necessary for knowing and understanding nature's law, they cannot be members of the state of full and equal liberty. Though children do not have this reason, Locke still recognizes that they possess the capacity to learn reason if properly educated or given the opportunity to mature to the age(s) of majority. In effect, this capacity for learning reason bestows upon children partial and conditional admittance to the state of full and equal liberty. Specifically, from birth until maturing to the age(s) of majority Locke's liberalism and therefore by implication the Constitution recognize that children possess the liberty to be preserved, nourished, and educated by their parents or by some guardian if their parents forfeit their parental obligation.

Thus, to enjoy either full or partial liberty, individuals must be born and possess reason or have the capacity to learn it. Therefore, assigning to the fetal-being a liberty interest in preservation, thereby preventing abortions from taking place except for health- and life-threatening reasons, requires that the development of the fetal-being has sufficiently progressed to the point that both pre-conditions are approximated within it. This means that the fetal-being must be sufficiently physiologically viable and brain developed to approximate a born child with the presumed capacity to learn reason. In short, before the fetal-being can possess a liberty interest in preservation, it must acquire both physiological and brain viability or humanness (Rubenfeld 1991).

A physiologically viable fetal-being is one that has "a reasonable potential for *subsequent survival*" if it were to be removed from the uterus (Lenow 1983, 10–emphasis in the original). Physiological viability makes the fetal-being approximately the same as a born child in that "subsequent survival" is also the same goal strived for by a full-term fetal-being that actually becomes the born child recognized in Locke's liberalism. Currently, physiological viability occurs somewhere between twenty-four and twenty-eight weeks of pregnancy (Grobstein 1988, 126). This occurrence depends upon the presence of pulmonary capability that generally is not in place until at least the twenty-third week of pregnancy (Rubenfeld 1991, 620). Without a sufficient degree of lung maturity and the ability for a fetal-being to breathe on its own or with mechanical assistance, the ability of a fetus to live for very long outside of the womb cannot be sustained. Thus, as defined here, physiological viability is akin to natural or near-natural viability wherein extensive medical resources are not generally needed to sustain the less than full-term fetal-being (Kennedy and Nicolazzo 1984-1985, 550).

Physiological viability is the first prong in pinpointing when the fetal-being acquires personhood and then has a liberty interest in preservation. Humanness is the second prong. As defined by one recent pair of commentators, humanness is the "possession of those properties that distinguish human beings from other living things. . . . [It] is defined . . . in purely biological terms and thus cannot vary from one culture to the next" (Morowitz and Trefil 1992, 16-17). These distinguishing properties usually occur with the "onset of the functioning of the cerebral cortex" (Morowitz and Trefil 1992, 17). At this stage of fetal growth, the fetal-being's brain has sufficiently matured to "begin to take on the cortical structure capable of higher mental functions" and "develops important attributes of the capacity for distinctly human mentality" (Rubenfeld 1991, 622, 624). In short, humanness can be thought of as equivalent to "brain viability."

Just when the cerebral cortex begins to function in ways that are uniquely human is open to some degree of disagreement. Some authorities assert that this advanced brain development generally occurs between the twenty-fourth and twenty-eighth weeks of pregnancy (Rubenfeld 1991, 622 fn. 108, 624 fn. 110; see also Reiter et al. 1991, 467). Others estimate the beginning of the functioning of the cerebral cortex to be between the twenty-fifth and thirty-second weeks of pregnancy (Morowitz and Trefil 1992, 119). Despite the lack of clear agreement, one thing is certain: based upon these estimates, the fetal-being cannot be in possession of the properties of humanness before at least the twenty-fourth week of pregnancy because the cerebral cortex is neither fully developed nor completely functioning in a totally human fashion before that time. Thus, the fetal-being cannot be recognized as possessing the unique properties of human beings any sooner than the twenty-fourth week of pregnancy. Therefore, only after this week can the fetal-being be like the Lockean child who does not know reason but nevertheless possesses the mental capability to learn it.

Taken together then, physiological viability and humanness or brain viability express that point at which the fetal-being approximates the Lockean-born child capable of learning reason. This recognition takes place no sooner than the twenty-fourth week of pregnancy and no later than the thirty-second week, or between the sixth and eighth month of pregnancy. It is at this nexus between physiological viability and humanness, then, that the fetal-being comes to possess the personhood necessary for asserting a liberty interest in preservation. It is at this juncture that the fetal-being not only possesses survivability but also can "in some important sense *live* as humans live" (Rubenfeld 1991, 623).

Though articulating two distinct dimensions for viability, requiring both physiological viability and humanness is not really radically different from the notion of viability set forth in *Roe* v. *Wade*. Rather, it merely better expresses one reasonable interpretation of *Roe*'s viability standard that generally has been disregarded and ignored. Post-*Roe* abortion cases have interpreted *Roe*'s viability standard exclusively in terms of survivability or physiological viability. For example, in *Planned Parenthood of Southeastern Pennsylvania* v. *Casey* (120 L. Ed. 2d 674 at 710), the plurality opinion of Justices O'Connor, Kennedy, and Souter defined viability as "the time at which there is a realistic possibility of maintaining and nourishing a life outside the womb."

Though routinely interpreted as meaning only physiological viability, the *Roe* majority did not write simply about survivability. Instead, it addressed viability as that point at which the fetal-being "presumably has the capability of *meaningful life* outside the mother's womb" (93 S. Ct. 705 at 732–emphasis added). Designating a "meaningful life" as an aspect of viability can be reasonably understood as a reference to and expectation of humanness or brain viability that enables the fetal-being to "*live* in some 'meaningful' human sense" (Rubenfeld 1991, 623–emphasis in the original).

In more clearly articulating *Roe*'s reference to humanness, the approach proposed here also overcomes the greatest shortcoming of the *Roe* definition of viability as it has come to be interpreted. The classic and most often cited criticism of *Roe* v. *Wade*'s statement of viability is that it is on a collision course with advances in medical technology that push back fetal survivability to earlier points in a pregnancy. The best known expression of this criticism is Justice O'Connor's dissent in *City of Akron* v. *Akron Center for Reproductive Health, Inc.* (76 L. Ed. 2d 687 at 720):

> Just as improvements in medical technology inevitably will move *forward* the point at which [government] may regulate for reasons of maternal health, different technological improvements will move *backward* the point of viability at which [government] may proscribe abortion. . . . In 1972 viability before 28 weeks was considered unusual. . . . However, recent studies have demonstrated increasingly earlier fetal viability. It is certainly reasonable to believe that fetal viability in the first of pregnancy may be possible in the not too distant future. . . . The *Roe* framework, then, is clearly on a collision course with itself.

This collision is inevitable if viability is understood only in terms of survivability or physiological viability. As Justice O'Connor noted in her *Akron* dissent, rapid advances in medical technology can push forward the point at which the fetal-being can become viable and survive outside of the womb. If viability means only physiological survivability, then as medical science advances the point of viability, the recognition of the fetal-being as a born person will occur earlier in the pregnancy. For example, advances in medical science may someday result in the fetal-being being viable from the point of conception through such means as an artificial womb or fetal transplants (Lenow 1983, 14; Tribe 1990, 220-223). If this day actually arrives, what today is recognized as a woman's liberty interest in the abortion decision will be altered greatly.

At least one commentator suggests that if medical science ever advances to the point where a fetal-being is viable from the moment of conception or some early stage of pregnancy, approaches to abortion policy that rely on the viability criterion must "do the right thing" and "accept the 'conservative' consequences of the viability criterion" (Zaitichik 1980, 22). This would mean the possibility of a complete prohibition on abortions. Others suggest that such medical advances would literally redefine the liberty interest in abortion from one primarily concerned with procreative choices to one in which the issue was a woman's right to control her own genetic material (Tribe 1990, 223-225).

But these issues arise only if physiological viability is the sole criterion of personhood. If the second Lockean-informed criterion of being able to learn reason is applied through a humanness standard, there is no collision. For even though advances in medical science may make it possible to achieve physiological viability at earlier points in fetal development, this viability would be insufficient to bestow personhood and a liberty interest in preservation upon the fetal-being because it would still lack the humanness or brain viability necessary to establish its capability for learning reason. Thus, rather than promoting fetal-being's personhood, such advances in medical science, if they do occur, would redefine the private procreative choices a woman possesses. Her range of choices would broaden to include continuing the pregnancy, abortion, or the removal of the pre-brain viable fetal-being and its transplant to either a surrogate mother or an artificial womb (if these are indeed the options resulting from advances in medical science).

Accepting, then, that the fetal-being's personhood and claim to a liberty interest in preservation begin no earlier than the point at which both physiological viability and humanness are achieved, has a definite and clear impact on both a woman's liberty interest in the abortion decision and government's ability to proscribe and regulate abortion. Before physiological viability and humanness, a woman's liberty interest in the abortion decision remains private and absolute. During this pre-viability stage, government is prohibited from taking any coercive action to prevent her from choosing abortion. Nevertheless, government may still try to influence the woman's abortion decisions through noncoercive means.

But at the nexus of physiological viability and humanness, the fetal-being's newly recognized liberty interest in preservation becomes superior to a woman's liberty interest in the abortion decision. From this point, a woman is limited in her action toward the fetal-being by the same restraints that would be placed upon her if the fetal-being were a born child with the capability of learning reason. She cannot exercise her liberty interest in abortion because to do so would fatally harm another individual with an equal liberty interest in preservation. In short, a woman's liberty interest in the abortion decision ends at the point in which the fetal-being achieves both physiological viability and humanness.

The one exception to this general rule is when the abortion of a viable fetal-being is necessary for preserving the health and life of the woman. As discussed earlier, Locke's liberalism does not require individuals to preserve others at the expense of their own life. Rather it only states that individuals should try and preserve others when their own preservation is not threatened. Thus, a woman experiencing a health- and life-threatening post-viability pregnancy must be allowed to terminate through abortion to preserve herself. But as will become clearer momentarily, even under this condition government does not surrender all interest in the post-viable life of the fetal-being.

Since at the nexus of physiological viability and humanness a woman's liberty interest in the abortion decision is diminished and the fetal-being's liberty interest in preservation becomes paramount, government must protect the fetal-being against harm. Indeed, because at the point of this physiological viability and humanness, the fetal-being has "capability for meaningful life outside the [woman's] womb," government regulation designed to secure its preservation is both "logically and biologically justified" (*Roe* v. *Wade*, 93 S. Ct. 705 at 732). In particular, government is obligated to use its coercive powers to secure the fetal-being's life by prohibiting all abortions except those necessary for preserving the health and life of the woman. But even for a medically necessary and life-preserving post-viability abortion, the fetal-being's interest in its own preservation is sufficient to require government to prescribe that such an abortion be performed through the method most likely to preserve the life of the fetal-being but does not significantly increase the risks to the woman's health or preservation.

In addition, the now equal status of the fetal-being and the woman justifies government action pertaining to the standard of care aborted post-viable fetal-beings receive. For example, the equal status of the fetal-being's liberty interest in preservation justifies such government regulations as requiring the attendance of a second physician when a physiological-viable and brain-viable fetal-being is aborted. In those post-viability abortions resulting in the live birth of the fetal-being, the second physician's sole concern is to preserve the life of the aborted but living fetal-being. As the Supreme Court recognized in *Planned Parenthood of Kansas City Missouri* v. *Ashcroft*,

> preserving the life of a viable [fetal-being] that is aborted may not often be possible, but the [government] legitimately may choose to provide safeguards for the comparatively few instances of live birth that do occur. . . . The second-physician requirement reasonably furthers [government's] compelling interest in protecting the lives of viable [fetal-beings]. (76 L. Ed. 2d 733 at 742)

Though physiological viability and humanness limit a woman's liberty interest in the abortion decision, from a Lockean-styled perspective this understanding of viability is still the best point at which to recognize a fetal-being's personhood and liberty interest in preservation for two important reasons. First, physiological viability and humanness are distinctions made by medical science. When both are likely to occur can be determined on the basis of objective, though admittedly somewhat imprecise and changing, medical criteria rather than on any moral or religious judgment. Using both, then, to recognize the fetal-being's interest in life keeps government from imposing any particular religious or moral belief onto the political community as to when life begins. In fact, incorporating into abortion policy any recognition of the fetal-being's life other than the understanding of viability presented here appears impermissible under the Lockean prohibition on imposing moral beliefs and behavior on those aspects of an individual's life assigned to the private sphere (*Roe* v. *Wade* 93 S. Ct. 705 at 730-731). For example, contrary to the plurality opinion in *Webster* v. *Reproductive Health Services* (106 L. Ed. 2d 410), the preamble of the Missouri statute claiming that "the life of each human being begins at conception" (106 L. Ed. 2d 410 at 426 quoting Missouri Revised Statutes sec. 1.205.1) is impermissible because it imposes a moral belief on the political community, a belief from which many dissent. As Justice Stevens writes in dissent, the preamble to the Missouri statute is "an unequivocal endorsement of a religious tenet of some but by no means all faiths" (106 L. Ed. 2d 410 at 467).

Second, recognition of the life of the fetal-being at the nexus of physiological viability and humanness most effectively maintains a balance between the fetal-being's interest in life and a woman's liberty interest in the abortion decision. This understanding of viability allows for neither of these conflicting interests to be sacrificed for the purpose of securing the other. Thus, recognizing the fetal-being's liberty interest in preservation from this point, although it limits a woman's liberty interest in abortion, helps to better secure this liberty interest. In this way, a viability standard based upon both physiological survivability and humanness actually allows for greater protection for a woman's liberty interest in the abortion decision, in a manner more constitutionally correct than the alternatives proposed by some past and current members of the Supreme Court. For example, dissenting in the *Thornburgh* case, Justice White wrote:

> The governmental interest at issue [in abortion] is in protecting those who will be citizens if their lives are not ended in the womb. The substantiality of this interest is in no way dependent on the probability that the fetus may be capable of surviving outside the womb at any given point in its development. . . . The State's interest is in the fetus as an entity in itself, and the character of this entity does not change at the point of viability. . . . Accordingly, the State's interest, if compelling after viability, is equally compelling before viability. (90 L. Ed. 2d 779 at 815-816)

In *Webster* v. *Reproductive Health Services*, Chief Justice Rehnquist, speaking for the Court's majority, wrote that he could "not see why the [government's] interest in protecting potential human life should come into existence only at the point of viability" (106 L. Ed. 2d 410 at 436). The outcome of alternatives such as those proposed by Justice White and Chief Justice Rehnquist is clearly evident. These alternatives do not distinguish between the private and public sphere when a woman's liberty interest in abortion is the issue. They would "return to the States virtually unfettered authority to control the quintessentially intimate, personal, and life-directing decision whether to carry a fetus to term" (*Webster* v. *Reproductive Health Services* 106 L. Ed. 2d 410 at 448– Justice Blackmun dissenting). They would permit an imposition of a morality upon women over aspects of their private lives with which many would not agree. In so doing, these alternatives would permit government "to conscript a woman's body and force upon her a 'distressful life and future' rather than a life over which she has come to believe the Constitution guaranteed her some control" (*Webster* v. *Reproductive Health Services* 106 L. Ed. 2d 410 at 461–Justice Blackmun dissenting). However, such actions would be totally contrary to the fundamental principles of Lockean-styled liberalism and its incorporation into the Constitution.

AN IMPLICATION BEYOND ABORTION

Assigning personhood to the fetal-being at the point of physiological viability and humanness carries with it an important implication beyond abortion for the relationship among a woman, the fetal-being, and government. It is an implication whose full meaning and impact upon this three-way relationship is beyond the scope of this current work. Nevertheless, its importance and relevance to the current discussion still require that it be discussed here in, at least, some limited manner.

If the nexus of physiological viability and humanness or brain viability is the point at which a fetal-being possesses personhood and a corresponding liberty interest in preservation that protects it against an elective post-viability abortion, then this same liberty interest in preservation must also protect the viable fetal-being from other forms of fetal abuse less severe than abortion but still likely to impinge upon its preservation. Thus, in addition to its obligation to proscribe all post-viability abortions except those necessary to preserve a woman's health or life, Lockean-styled government would appear obligated to regulate and restrict the otherwise private behavior of a woman carrying a post-viable fetal-being that risks injury to it or endangers its preservation. Indeed, if the viable fetal-being is to be secure in its liberty interest in preservation, then

---

*As this book went to press, Justice White announced his retirement effective June 1993. However, rather than rewrite this portion of the discussion, I decided to retain the original text to underscore just how tenuous a woman's liberty interest in the abortion decision was during the time this book was being written. It remains to be seen how Justice White's replacement will effect what the Supreme Court's constitutional understanding of this liberty interest will become.

this authority is but a logical and necessary extension of government's authority to proscribe elective post-viable abortions.

The justification for both is the same: nature's law against individuals using their liberty in ways that are harmful to others. Enforcement of this law is an original reason for forming government. In recognizing this law, Lockean-styled liberalism does not allow government to be selective when it come to choosing what threats to their preservation to protect individuals against. It has no discretion on this point. Rather its obligation is to secure for individuals their preservation against all threats arising from the actions of other individuals. Thus, it is only through the authority to regulate the otherwise private behavior of a pregnant woman threatening the preservation of the viable fetal-being that enables government to secure for it this liberty beyond abortion.

Nature's law against exercising liberty in ways harmful to other persons is one pillar on which Lockean-styled government's ability to regulate and restrict the otherwise private behavior of a woman pregnant with a viable fetal-being rests. The nature of parental authority and obligation derived from Lockean-styled liberalism is the second pillar supporting this authority. From a Lockean point of view, the relationship between a pregnant woman and a viable fetal-being can be understood as being somewhat analogous to the relationship between a born child and his or her parents. Specifically, at the nexus of physiological viability and humanness or brain viability, the Lockean parental obligations to nourish and preserve the child are fully in place and operable as if the fetal-being were a born child. Thus, in failing or choosing not to abort the fetal-being before viability, the pregnant woman, whether willingly or not, has pressed upon her these Lockean obligations to nourish and preserve the fetal-being. And like the Lockean parents of a born child, this obligation is "so incumbent on [her] for [the viable fetal-being's] good, that nothing can absolve [her] from taking care of [it]" (*Second Treatise*, sec. 67).

Since biologically the pregnant woman and the viable fetal-being have not yet been separated from one another, the latter, like a born child, is completely dependent upon her for its nourishment and preservation, the pregnant woman choosing to act responsibly in regard to her parental obligations has no choice but to refrain from otherwise private behavior that is potentially harmful to a viable fetal-being or threatening to its preservation. For a woman pregnant with a viable fetal-being to act otherwise and engage in behavior harmful or threatening to its preservation would be equivalent to possessing absolute control over its life and death. As discussed in Chapter 5, absolute control over the life and death of their children is a power Lockean-styled liberalism recognizes that parents do not possess any more than legitimate government possesses absolute control over the members of the political community in whose name it governs. Instead, parents acting so or in other ways harmful to their children forfeit their parental authority over them. This authority, then, transfers to government or its designate.

Accordingly, a pregnant woman engaging in otherwise private behavior that places the preservation of her viable fetal-being at risk effectively "quits" the care of it. In so doing, she forfeits her parental authority over and obligations to the fetal-being. As with the forfeiture of parental authority over a born child, the parental authority of the pregnant woman over a viable fetal-being would appear to be transferred to government. This transfer of parental authority from the pregnant woman to government requires the authority to regulate and restrict her otherwise private behavior. The physical union between the woman and the fetal-being calls for this. It is only through this temporary regulating and restraining of the pregnant woman and her otherwise private behavior that government can secure the preservation of a viable fetal-being against a pregnant woman who, if left alone, would presumably continue to abuse the fetal-being and threaten its preservation.

At first glance, a Lockean recognition of fetal rights beyond abortion and government's corresponding authority to regulate and restrain a pregnant woman's behavior appears severely restrictive of and intrusive into her private life. As one commentator observes,

> allowing the government to impose special penalties and restrictions on pregnant women's actions in order to promote asserted interest in the fetus would, if left unchecked, enable the government virtually to dictate how pregnant women must live their lives. (Johnsen 1989, 180)

Contrary to such concerns, a Lockean recognition of fetal rights actually protects a pregnant woman's private life by providing a balanced approach between her liberty and the viable fetal-being's liberty interest in preservation. This is because unlike most contemporary approaches to fetal rights, a Lockean approach recognizes limits upon both when the claim of fetal rights can be made and the extent to which government can exercise its authority to regulate a pregnant woman's otherwise private behavior in order to secure the preservation of a viable fetal-being. In so doing, it effectively responds to the critics of fetal rights who claim that "fetal-rights advocates grant fetuses more rights than women" (Pollitt 1990, 414).

A Lockean-informed understanding of fetal rights, therefore, is superior to, less excessive, and less intrusive than the approach to fetal rights espoused by many contemporary fetal-rights activists. First, the Lockean perspective conditions a claim of fetal rights on the fetal being securing personhood. This has been defined here as the nexus of physiological and brain viability. In contrast, contemporary discussions of fetal rights fail to clearly distinguish between the pre-viable and viable fetal-being. For example, Margery Shaw, one of the nation's leading fetal-rights advocates, would extend fetal rights to the fetal-being almost from conception. She writes: "Every woman should consider herself pregnant on the first day her period was due and avoid exposure to anything that has been implemented in birth defects" (Shaw 1984, 73). In response, liberal feminist critics of this perspective argue that imposing such severe restrictions on a pregnant woman's activities "implies that there is a 'rights status' for an entity that has not yet come into being" and that it "places the rights of a hypothetical entity above those of a live rights-bearer" (Losco 1991, 11).

This failure or unwillingness to assign fetal rights to distinguish between pre-viable and viable fetal-beings sets up a badly flawed logic that a woman who is "willingly pregnant," having chosen birth over abortion, is subject to having her otherwise private behavior regulated throughout her pregnancy rather than just from viability, as the Lockean perspective allows. This position maintains that "once a woman decides to bear a child, [government] has a compelling interest in protecting the fetus which justifies restrictions on her freedom" (Baer 1991, 12). Government can go as far as to impose upon the willingly pregnant woman a legal duty to ensure that the fetal-being is born as healthy as possible (Baer 1991, 12). Applying this reasoning to fetal surgery, the argument for restricting "willingly pregnant" women's behavior on behalf of the not yet viable fetal-being appears something like the passage quoted below:

> Where the mother expresses the desire to carry the [fetal-being] to term and yet refuses to consent to surgical procedures beneficial to the fetus . . . forcing fetal surgery would not impinge the mother's right to decide whether or not to have the child, but only her decision to condemn the child to a life with handicaps. While it is certainly arguable that the mother's privacy rights are equally infringed whether one is restricting her right to abort or her right to refuse to consent to fetal surgery, the latter presents a situation where a living, breathing person will come into existence suffering from handicaps which could have been prevented. (Lenow 1983, 23)

As the above passage makes clear, under this idea of being "willingly pregnant," a pregnant woman pursuing birth would indeed enjoy less liberty than a woman choosing to abort. Upon her decision to remain pregnant, her otherwise private behavior can be restrained throughout the duration of her pregnancy. But a woman considering abortion would have her liberty constrained only if she failed to secure an abortion before physiological and brain viability. In effect, this contemporary perspective on fetal rights produces an unacceptable inequality between the liberty enjoyed by a pregnant woman considering abortion and one who chooses birth. Thus, by allowing for a pregnancy-long incursion into her liberty, this contemporary perspective on fetal rights actually punishes a woman for choosing birth over abortion. This leaves acting "as if" she intends to abort as her only means to escape the impositions of these controls over her private behavior.

The Lockean perspective on fetal rights discussed above does not allow for such inequalities to exist between pregnant women who choose to abort and those who choose to continue their pregnancies. Rather, since it distinguishes between a pre-viable and viable fetal-being, under the Lockean orientation to fetal rights, a pregnant woman is subject to government regulation and restriction after viability only when abortion is no longer permissible except for health reasons or to preserve the woman's life. Before viability, though it may conclude that a pregnant woman has a moral obligation to behave in ways not threatening to the preservation of the fetal-being she intends to bring to term, government cannot impose that moral obligation upon her. Its authority to act against the woman and on behalf of the fetal-being only occurs at that point at which the fetal-being attains personhood and the liberty associated with it. Before this point, government's interest is only in the potential life of the fetal-being. This is an interest it must pursue, like any other member of the political community, through such noncoercive means as moral suasion. That government is restricted from taking coercive action against a pregnant woman before the fetal-being attains personhood is one aspect of the "price and prize" of Lockean liberalism discussed in Chapter 2.

Conditioning government regulation of a pregnant woman's otherwise private behavior on the fetal-being achieving both physiological and brain viability is one way in which a Lockean approach to fetal rights beyond abortion differs from the contemporary perspective. A second way this approach differs is that the Lockean-styled perspective presented here also more evenly balances the competing interests between a woman and the fetal-being; this is done by limiting what otherwise private behavior of a pregnant woman government can regulate and restrict. Since the extension of personhood and liberty to the fetal-being are premised upon its approximation to a born child, the otherwise private behavior of the pregnant woman that government can restrict and regulate must have a direct or near approximation to impermissible actions against a born child. Thus, applying existing child-neglect laws to alleged instances of fetal abuse is one way to ascertain impermissible actions against a viable fetal-being. For example, under most conventional understandings of child neglect, parents are not at liberty to refuse essential medical care for their children. "Consequently, a pregnant woman who has chosen to go to term cannot refuse care necessary for the well-being of her [viable fetal-being]. To decline such care [for it] is the equivalent of child neglect" (Phillips 1991,

419). Some state governments already approximate this criterion of defining and limiting fetal abuse in terms of equivalent or near-equivalent forms of abuse against a born child. It primarily is accomplished through the "born alive" standard wherein if the fetal-being is born alive, a woman is held accountable and punishable for fetal abuses, such as fetal alcohol syndrome or fetal drug addiction. For example, "nineteen states now have laws that allow child abuse charges to be made against women who give birth to a child with illegal drugs in his/her bloodstream" (Losco 1991, 4).

Admittedly, the "direct analogy" standard suggested by a Lockean-informed perspective of fetal rights would subject a pregnant woman who is neglectful in the care of or abusive toward the viable fetal-being to possible criminal prosecution or either the temporary or permanent forfeiture of parental authority. But in narrowing the definition of fetal abuse to actions and behavior analogous to those taken against a born child, this Lockean-inspired criterion guards against a woman being held responsible for fetal abuse occurring outside of her control. For example, under this standard, a woman could not be held responsible for physical and mental defects to a fetal-being resulting from physician-prescribed medications or other medical procedures recommended or required by her obstetrician. In drawing this distinction, a Lockean-informed approach to recognizing fetal rights moves a pregnant woman's responsibility away from the extreme position taken by some fetal-rights advocates who claim that the "production of an imperfect newborn should make a woman liable to criminal charges and 'wrongful life' suits if she knows, or should have known the risk involved in her behavior" that ultimately affected the fetal-being (Pollitt 1990, 415).

In addition, the Lockean-styled approach to fetal rights drawn from this discussion also makes certain that a pregnant woman carrying a viable fetal-being is not held up to higher legal standards than parents of a born child are. For example, existing child-abuse statutes throughout the United States assign the principal responsibility for the health, welfare, and safety of their children to the parents. But these statutes and the enforcement of them do not hold parents responsible for a "perfect environment" but "only with not taking irresponsible actions or failing to follow responsible standards of care" (Losco 1989, 274).

Finally, while the above discussion has centered on the viable fetal-being being free from actions of the pregnant woman that might harm it, the perspective presented here also recognizes that the viable fetal-being additionally must be protected from individuals who assist a pregnant woman in her abusive behavior against it. This recognition is premised on a basic logic that "there is no reason why pregnant women should be singled out for actions that they may not have committed alone" (Losco 1991, 18). Thus, individuals who sell or give illegal drugs to a woman pregnant with a viable fetal-being or sell her alcohol would be equally as guilty and punishable on the grounds of fetal abuse as she would be.

Second, this Lockean-styled perspective recognizes that the viable fetal-being must also be protected from individuals who commit physical attacks upon the pregnant woman and in the course of those attacks harm it, too. Even though a fetal-being enjoys the same legal status as a born child once it acquires physiological viability and humanness, it is not yet biologically separate from the pregnant woman; it is still physically connected to and dependent upon her for life support. Therefore, any physical attack on the pregnant woman not only threatens her preservation but also that of the fetal-being. It is as if two separate attacks occurred. In both cases, the relevant criminal statute could be applied. For example, the man who commits spousal abuse on a woman pregnant with a viable fetal-being also commits child abuse upon the fetal-being, and under the Lockean-styled approach to fetal rights presented here, he can be prosecuted and punished for two separate crimes. The same would be true for individuals charged with the vehicular manslaughter of a pregnant woman carrying a viable fetal-being. Such individuals could be charged with two rather than just one count of the crime. Therefore, recognizing the need to preserve the viable fetal-being from individuals other than just the pregnant woman is an effective response to fetal-rights critics who charge that fetal-rights advocates generally impose responsibility and criminality on only the woman (Pollitt 1990, 415). But under the Lockean-informed approach discussed here, government has the authority to prosecute and punish all individuals who threaten the preservation of a viable fetal-being.

7

The Freedom of Choice Act

As discussed in the Preface, one of the purposes for developing and presenting the Lockean-styled middle perspective on abortion set forth here is to prove to policy-makers that abortion policy should be formulated from a clear understanding of how constitutional theory limits both the liberty interest in the abortion decision and government restrictions on that liberty. To draw closer attention to this point, this chapter analyzes from the Lockean-styled perspective developed in the preceding chapters the amended version of the Freedom of Choice Act introduced into but not passed by the 101 and 102 Congress. In so doing, the hope and purpose of this analysis is to demonstrate both the practicality of this Lockean perspective and how it can be used to both construct and evaluate abortion policy.

The Freedom of Choice Act was first introduced into the House of Representatives and the Senate as HR 3700 and S 1921, respectively, on November 17, 1989, late in the second session of the 101 Congress (Congressional Quarterly Staff November 25, 1989, 3241). Though the House Judiciary Committee Subcommittee on Civil and Constitutional Rights approved the legislation, the 101 Congress adjourned before the full House Judiciary Committee could consider the bill and before either of the two full chambers could take final action (Rovner June 20, 1992, 1808).

Reintroduced in the first session of the 102 Congress as HR 25 and S 25, the substantive content of the Freedom of Choice Act was the same as its 1989 predecessor. It also was quite brief, just a single page in length and consisting of just nineteen lines of text. In terse and spartan language, HR 25 stated:

Except as provided in subsection (b), a State may not restrict the right of a woman to choose to terminate a pregnancy—

(1) before fetal viability; or

(2) at any time, if such termination is necessary to protect the life or health of the woman.

(b) . . . A State may impose requirements medically necessary to protect the life or health of women referred to in subsection (a).

Through these few words, the ninety-first House and twenty-second Senate sponsors of the act sought "to establish in Federal statutory law the same limitations upon the power of the States to restrict the freedom of women to terminate a pregnancy as existed under the strict scrutiny standard of review enunciated in *Roe* v. *Wade* . . . and applied in subsequent cases" until *Webster* v. *Reproductive Health Services* (Senate Committee on Labor and Human Resources 1992, 3). According to Senator Alan Cranston (D–California), one of the Act's Senate sponsors, the legislation had one simple goal: to "preserve the rights of women to make their own personal decisions without government interference" (Rovner July 11, 1992, 2046).

As Senator Cranston's words suggest, pro-choice frustration over the seemingly anti-choice Supreme Court decisions in *Webster* v. *Reproductive Health Services* and *Planned Parenthood of Southeastern Pennsylvania* v. *Casey*, which allowed greater state restriction of abortion and abortion-related services, contributed to the genesis of the Freedom of Choice Act. For example, this pro-choice concern over *Webster* and *Casey's* restrictive natures was readily apparent in a supporting report submitted on July 1, 1992, by the Senate Committee on Labor and Human Resources and in its favorable reporting of the Act (S 25) on July 1, 1992. In explaining the need for the Freedom of Choice Act, the Committee majority wrote:

. . . The Supreme Court stands today only one vote away from overruling *Roe* and adopting a rationality test which would approve all restrictions on abortion including absolute bans. Four justices dissented in *Casey* and asserted that they would overrule *Roe* without regard to consideration of precedent and *stare decisis* and would allow a State to regulate abortion in any way as long as there was a "rational basis" for the law. Thus, the need for the Freedom of Choice Act cannot be seen simply in light of the standards enunciated in *Casey* but also in light of the imminent danger that the Supreme Court will overrule *Roe* and adopt a rational basis test which would allow a State to ban abortion. (Senate Committee on Labor and Human Resources 1992, 13)

Regardless of the concern pro-choice members of Congress expressed about recent anti-abortion court decisions, politics, particularly election-year politics, also was important to the genesis of the Freedom of Choice Act. Indeed, supporters of the bill generally admitted that the short-term goal of the act was "more political than legislative" (Rovner July 4, 1992, 1951). For example, pro-choice supporters of the 1989 version of the legislation targeted the 1990 congressional elections. They hoped to use the bill as a means of electing a veto-proof, pro-choice majority to the 102 Congress (Congressional Quarterly Staff November 25, 1989, 3241). The supporters of the 1991 incarnation of the act had both congressional and presidential politics in mind as they worked for its passage. Regarding the former, "backers . . . want[ed] to force members [of Congress] to say once and for all whether they support[ed] a woman's right to have an abortion" (Rovner August 1, 1992, 2286). This was something neither chamber of Congress had ever done.

But the principal political target supporters of the 1991 Freedom of Choice Act had in their electoral gun sights was George Bush, the incumbent president. Knowing that even if the act passed in both houses of Congress it would face on inevitable presidential veto, pro-choice Democrats in Congress wanted to use that veto to help their party's presidential candidate in the 1992 fall election (Rovner July 4, 1992, 1951). Sensing that President Bush's strict pro-life stand was becoming a political albatross around his neck, these Democratic members of Congress planned to "force him to veto a raft of bills relaxing federal restrictions on [abortion] . . . The Freedom of Choice Act . . . was to be the cherry atop the sundae" (Rovner August 1, 1992, 2286). Indeed, pro-choice Republicans publicly supported the bill in hopes of getting President Bush to soften a rigid anti-abortion position that was not only hurting himself electorally but also congressional Republicans in general (Rovner July 4, 1992, 1951).

The pungent aroma of electoral politics rising from the Freedom of Choice Act made some observers and participants in the abortion controversy question congressional Democrats' sincerity as to whether or not they actually wanted to see the Freedom of Choice Act passed and signed into law. For example, Tanya Melich, the executive director of the New York State Republican Family Committee, stated in a *New York Times* editorial (July 30, 1992) that a look at the Democratic party's record on abortion "invites cynicism." She noted that "the Democrats have been partners in many of the actions that have caused American women to lose their reproductive freedom" (Melich July 30, 1992, A25). In particular, she pointed out a Democratic Congress that passed the Hyde Amendment, which prohibited Medicaid-financed abortions for impoverished women. Perhaps more damning, Melich pointed to the Democratic House leadership's timidity in trying to muster the necessary votes to override President Bush's veto of other congressional attempts to liberalize federal abortion policy. As evidence of this timidity, she turned to the House's failure to override President Bush's veto of the National Institute of Health authorization bill, which allowed federal financing of the fetal-tissue research. She notes that during this debate,

> Speaker Tom Foley . . . seemed uninvolved. David Bonior of Michigan, the majority party whip, was one of the seven non-voting Democrats. . . . Richard Gephardt of Missouri, the House majority leader, worked hard, but one out of three is not a full-court press. (Melich July 30, 1992, A25)

Congressional action on the 1992 incarnation of the Freedom of Choice Act somewhat substantiated Melich's cynicism toward the congressional Democratic leadership's legislative commitment to the bill. Amended versions of the Freedom of Choice Act (HR 25 and S 25) were approved by the House Judiciary Committee and the Senate Labor and Resources Committee on June 30, 1992 and July 1, 1992, respectively. Both committees approved their version of the act with strong support from a majority of their committee members. The House Judiciary Committee approved its amended version with a 20 to 13 vote. The Senate Labor and Human Resources Committee approved its version with a 12 to 5 vote (Rovner July 4, 1992, 1951). But after committee approval, which occurred just before the 1992 Democratic National Convention, both the House and Senate Democratic leadership allowed the amended versions of the Freedom of Choice Act to languish on the House and Senate legislative dockets. This happened even after the Senate version was amended to address some concerns raised by Senate Majority Leader George Mitchell over the constitutionality of the act and in spite of the fact that the Senate Majority Leader had publicly stated the need for congressional action. In July 1992 and in the immediate aftermath of the *Casey* decision, Mitchell publicly stated: "The Congress must act to ensure that the fundamental right of American women to choose for themselves is not lost. . . . " (Rovner July 4, 1992, 1951).

Despite Senator Mitchell's strong public pronouncement, by August 1992 neither he nor Speaker Foley had scheduled floor action in their respective chambers on the Freedom of Choice Act. Publicly, they were still insisting that full House and Senate consideration of the act would take place before the August 1992 Republican National Convention (Rovner August 1, 1992, 2286). This promised action never materialized, and the 1991-1992 incarnation of the Freedom of Choice Act suffered the same fate as the 1989 version. The 102 Congress adjourned before the full House and Senate could consider it. Two more years later, the act was no closer to being enacted. Why this occurred is largely speculative. One possible explanation rests in the *Casey* opinion not actually overturning *Roe* v.

Wade. "The lack of a dramatic overturn meant that there would be no firestorm of outrage to propel the legislation" forward toward successful passage (Rovner July 4, 1992, 1051). In addition, the political mileage Democrats hoped to get from a presidential veto of the bill became less important to the presidential contest as Democratic party nominee Bill Clinton continued to lead President Bush in the pre-election polls and began to secure an electoral-college lock on the election.

ANALYZING THE FREEDOM OF CHOICE ACT

At the time of this writing, the 103 Congress has yet to pass a 1994 version of the Freedom of Choice Act. Nevertheless, an analysis of the marked-up and amended 1991-1992 versions of the act approved by the House Judiciary Committee and the Senate Labor and Human Resources Committee still can provide a useful example of how to apply the Lockean-styled perspective on abortion developed in earlier chapters. For the purpose of this analysis, an abbreviated and composite Freedom of Choice Act is created from the amended versions of HR 25 and S 25. Only portions of both amended bills pertinent to applying the Lockean-styled perspective presented in preceding chapters are incorporated into this composite. Other substantive sections of the amended bills pertaining to such sections as Senate findings regarding Congress's constitutional authority to pass the act are excluded. These findings do present some interesting questions about the meaning of federalism and Congress's authority to regulate commerce. However, such questions are beyond the focus of this current work. Allowing for the above qualifiers, then, the substance of the Freedom of Choice Act constructed from amended versions of HR 25 and S 25 for use in this analysis reads as follows:

SEC. 2 RIGHT TO CHOOSE

(a) Except as provided in subsection (b), a State may not restrict the right of a woman to choose to terminate a pregnancy—

(1) before fetal viability; (HR 25) or

(2) at any time, if such termination is necessary to protect the life or health of the woman. (HR 25)

(b) . . . A State may impose requirements medically necessary to protect the life or health of women referred to in subsection (a) (HR 25)

(c) Rules of construction—Nothing in this Act shall be construed to:

(1) prevent a State from protecting unwilling individuals from having to participate in the performance of abortion to which they are conscientiously opposed; (HR 25)

(2) prevent a State from requiring a minor to involve a parent, guardian, or other responsible adult before terminating a pregnancy; (HR 25)

(3) prevent a State from declining to pay for the performance of abortions. (S 25)

Based upon the Lockean-styled perspective of a woman's liberty interest in the abortion decision developed in earlier chapters, the substantive provisions of the amended Freedom of Choice Act appear to incorporate some minimal Lockean-styled understanding. For example, the act is based at least upon an implicit recognition that decisions pertaining to abortion reside in the private sphere of human existence generally beyond the control and direction of government. That it is so premised, though, is due less to any serious reconsideration of the liberty interest and more to the limited legislative purpose of the act.

As previously noted, the legislative purpose of the Freedom of Choice Act seeks only to codify *Roe*, "thus freezing in place the state of abortion law up to but not including *Webster*" and *Casey* (Rovner July 4, 1992, 1952). In effect, then, the act seeks to do no more than codify conventional abortion orthodoxy but with a pro-choice hue. And as discussed in Chapter 4, by incorporating a degree of moral tolerance, the conventional pro-choice position on abortion approximates in some limited way a Lockean point of view. Beyond this, though, the incorporation of a Lockean-styled perspective in the Freedom of Choice Act must be judged incomplete and inadequate. A section-by-section analysis of the act helps to underscore this conclusion.

One of the most readily available examples of the act's failure to incorporate a Lockean-styled perspective is evident in Section 2a(1), which states: ". . . a State may not restrict the right of a woman to choose to terminate a pregnancy—(1) before fetal viability." Though not defined in the act, fetal viability apparently means the conventional interpretation of *Roe*'s viability standard. A report on the Freedom of Choice Act filed by the Senate Committee on Labor and Human Resources clearly acknowledges this. Citing *Roe* v. *Wade* as its authoritative source, the report states: "Fetal viability is a medical determination concerning when a fetus can survive outside the womb albeit with artificial means" (Senate Committee on Labor and Human Resources 1992, 4).

As pointed out in Chapter 6, from a Lockean perspective, this definition of fetal viability is incomplete. A complete definition of fetal viability consists of two dimensions: the physiological viability, reflected in the act's definition, plus humanness or brain viability. By failing to acknowledge the humanness component of fetal viability, the Freedom of Choice Act actually undermines a woman's liberty interest in abortion by tying it too closely to the state of medical science—a charge also legitimately leveled against *Roe*. The act's definition of viability, like that of the *Roe* decision from which it is drawn, guarantees that the statutory grant of liberty recognized by it is on a "collision course with itself" (*City of Akron* v. *Akron Center for Reproductive Health, Inc.* 76 L. Ed. 2d 687 at 720–Justice O'Connor dissenting).

The Freedom of Choice Act's incorporation of only physiological viability also speaks to the act's lack of concern and unwillingness to address the crucial and, eventually, unavoidable issue of when the fetal-being acquires personhood and a liberty interest in preservation equal to that of the woman seeking to terminate her unwanted pregnancy. In refusing to confront the issue of fetal-being personhood, the act clearly demonstrates the liberal excesses of the conventional pro-choice position. This is because by refusing to address this issue, the act cannot provide any real and meaningful balance between the eventual competing liberty interests of the woman and the fetal-being involved, as required by the Lockean-styled perspective presented in this study. The Freedom of Choice Act can accomplish this balance only by applying the two prongs of viability suggested by a Lockean understanding presented in Chapter 6. It is at the nexus of physiological viability and humanness that the fetal-being by definition acquires personhood and the accompanying liberty interest in preservation. It is also at this point of personhood that the fetal-being's liberty interest in preservation supersedes a woman's liberty interest in the abortion decision, except when continuing the pregnancy poses a serious risk to her health or life. In any statutory effort to recognize a liberty interest in abortion, Lockean-styled liberalism requires that these limits on that liberty also be acknowledged. Nevertheless, the Freedom of Choice Act fails to acknowledge any of this.

The Freedom of Choice Act comes a bit closer to a Lockean-styled perspective on abortion in Section 2(a)(2) and Section 2(b). Both sections reflect and seek to secure a woman's liberty interest in preservation. Section 2(b) of the act clearly states this concern. It reads: "A State may impose requirements medically necessary to protect the life or health of women referred to in subsection (a)." However, while the wording in Section 2(a)(2) is equally clear, overall it is insufficient. As with Section 2(a)(1), it stipulates a condition under which state government cannot restrict a woman's access to abortion. Specifically, it stipulates that state governments cannot restrict a woman's access to abortion "if such termination is necessary to protect the life or health of the mother." But in securing a woman's liberty interest in preservation, the act refuses to acknowledge that in most cases in which a pregnancy becomes life-threatening, the fetal-being will have acquired personhood and, thus, possess its own liberty interest in preservation equal to that of the woman.

In so doing, the act errs by failing to recognize that even if a woman seeks to abort a viable fetal-being to serve her own preservation, this choice of action by no means negates the soon-to-be-aborted fetal-being's own liberty interest in preservation. To the contrary, by choosing to abort a viable fetal-being in possession of personhood, the woman acting to secure her own preservation forfeits whatever authority she has over the fetal-being. But the exercise of this choice can by no means minimize or negate the viable fetal-being's liberty interest in preservation or the need to have this preservation secured for it by a guardian of some sort. When a woman forfeits her guardianship of the fetal-being, this authority and corresponding responsibility for preserving the fetal-being are transferred to another. In this instance, when a pregnant woman invokes her liberty interest in preservation, the authority to preserve the viable fetal-being is transferred to government. The government must work to secure that preservation for the soon-to-be-aborted fetal-being. This happens because Lockean-styled liberalism recognizes that "Nature has laid on Man as well as other creatures [the duty] to preserve their Off-spring, till they be able to shift for themselves" (*Second Treatise*, sec. 60). As noted in both Chapters 2 and 6, the one exception to this duty appears to be when a parent's own preservation is also at risk (*Second Treatise*, sec. 6). A life-threatening pregnancy is one such instance.

To briefly repeat part of the relevant discussion in Chapter 6 (pages 95-96):

> Since at the nexus of physiological viability and humanness a woman's liberty interest in the abortion decision is diminished and the fetal-being's liberty interest in preservation becomes paramount, government must protect the fetal-being against harm. Indeed, *since at the point of this physiological viability and humanness*, the fetal-being has "capability for meaningful life outside the [woman's] womb," government regulation designed to secure its preservation are both logically and biologically justified (*Roe* v. *Wade*, 93 S. Ct. 705 at 732). . . . [E]ven for a medically necessary and life preserving post-viability abortion, the fetal-being's interest in its own preservation is sufficient to require government to prescribe that such an abortion be performed through the method most likely to preserve the life of the fetal-being but does not significantly increase the risks to the woman's health or preservation. In addition, the now equal status of the fetal-being and the woman justifies government action pertaining to the standard of care aborted post-viable fetal-beings receive. For example, the equal status of the fetal-being's liberty interest in preservation justifies government regulations such as requiring the attendance of a second physician when a physiological and brain viable fetal-being is aborted. In those post-viability

abortions resulting in the live birth of the fetal-being, the second physician's sole concern would be preserving the life of the aborted but living fetal-being.

But in a display of pro-choice excesses, the Freedom of Choice Act fails to address any of these issues surrounding the viable fetal-being's liberty interest in preservation and government's responsibility for taking appropriate actions to secure it.

The composite version of the Freedom of Choice Act constructed from amended versions of HR 25 and S 25 also includes three rules of construction. The third rule is perhaps the section of the Freedom of Choice Act displaying the greatest of compatibility with the Lockean-styled perspective developed in the earlier chapters. Section 2(c)(3) stipulates that nothing in the act shall be interpreted to "prevent a State from declining to pay for the performance of abortions." Through its inclusion, the Freedom of Choice Act acknowledges that, like all Lockean-styled liberty, a woman's liberty interest in the abortion decision is an expression of negative rather than positive freedom. It is the liberty

to be free from government forced or coerced moral choices about how best to resolve her unwanted pregnancy. . . . It does not impose any positive obligation on government to secure for [her] the ability to actually exercise or act on her private moral choice to resolve her unwanted pregnancy through abortion. (Chapter 4 at 45)

In contrast, the second rule of construction provided for in the Freedom of Choice Act reflects less of the Lockean-styled perspective developed throughout the preceding chapters than does the first rule. Section 2(c)(2) states that nothing in the act shall be interpreted to "prevent a state from requiring a minor to involve a parent, guardian, or other responsible adult before terminating a pregnancy." This rule of construction is problematic for two reasons. First, it is overly inclusive. It fails to exempt from the requirement of parental consent those minor women who have reached the age of presumed reason concerning an independent liberty interest in the abortion decision. Second, Section 2(c)(2) does not exempt from parental consent those minor women under the age of presumed reason who are experiencing life-threatening pregnancies or who are pregnant as a result of incest rape.

The first rule of construction, though, is perhaps the most interesting and the one likely to generate the most controversy and conflict if implemented in the manner currently proposed. Section 2(c)(1) states that "[n]othing in this Act shall be construed to . . . prevent a State from protecting unwilling individuals from having to participate in the performance of abortions to which they are conscientiously opposed" [HR 25, Sec. 2(c)(1)]. Through this stipulation, this rule of construction recognizes that freedom of choice is a "two-way street." One side of the street is the woman's liberty to choose whether or not to terminate an unwanted pregnancy by having an abortion. The other side of the street is the liberty of health-care professionals who possess the medical expertise necessary to perform or assist in the performance of an abortion, to make the private moral choice whether or not to do so. By acknowledging both sides of the street, the Freedom of Choice Act recognizes that government cannot allow one individual's private moral choices to be fulfilled at the expense or sacrifice of those moral choices of another individual. To the contrary, this provision recognizes that the opposite is true. Government must act to guarantee that this does not happen.

In so stating, Section 2(c)(1) acknowledges that government is absent the power to compel health-care professionals to perform any abortion to which they are morally opposed. To do otherwise violates the Lockean-styled distinction between the private and public sphere of human existence and the Lockean-styled principle of moral tolerance without moral indifference. Thus, a pro-choice government requiring by statute that health-care professionals perform abortions to which they are morally opposed would not be a display of moral indifference. It would speak loudly to that government's preferred moral position. But such actions would lack moral tolerance. In accomplishing its moral position, the pro-choice government would be using its coercive power to forcibly extract moral behavior from individuals who would freely choose to behave otherwise.

Though the Freedom of Choice Act recognizes the two-way street of abortion, doing so through a mere rule of construction is insufficient from the Lockean-styled perspective developed in earlier chapters. As a mere rule of construction, Section 2(c)(1) only clarifies meaning. It neither protects or instructs other levels of government to protect health-care professionals regarding their private moral choices about participating in the performance of an abortion. Without a provision of this nature, the Freedom of Choice Act cannot truly protect the two forms of choice inherent in abortion: the choice of the woman seeking to terminate an unwanted pregnancy and the choice of anti-abortion health care professionals. Failing to do this, the Freedom of Choice Act cannot reflect completely the Lockean-styled understanding of the liberty interest in abortion preceding chapters have argued is constitutionally required of it.

Second, even if this revision were instituted, Section 2(c)(1) would still be insufficient because it protects only health-care professionals placed in the position of choosing whether or not to participate in the actual performance of an abortion. It fails to protect both private-sector, anti-abortion health-care administrators and health-care organizations built, in part, upon an anti-abortion philosophy. By excluding these health care administrators and organizations, Section 2(c)(1) suggests that a government choosing to pursue a vigorous pro-choice position could do so by requiring all private hospitals or health care clinics to perform abortions as long as health-care professionals morally opposed to abortions were exempted from participating in the actual performance of them. But such a scenario would leave private-sector, anti-abortion health-care administrators and religion-based health-care organizations, such as hospitals operated by the Catholic Church, in the position of having to administer a government-required pro-choice policy to which they are morally opposed.

By failing to protect the private morality of these health-care administrators and organizations, Section 2(c)(1) errs on two counts. First, by ignoring the private morality of anti-abortion health-care administrators, Section 2(c)(1) creates a situation wherein private-sector, morally opposed third parties might be statutorily required to implement government pro-choice policy. As presented in Chapter 4 in the discussion of the Department of Health and Human Services abortion counseling gag rule, such government use of private-sector third parties is impermissible under the Lockean-styled interpretation of liberty developed in earlier chapters. What was written in Chapter 4 against the Department of Health and Human Services gag rule is equally true about the forced implementation of pro-choice abortion policy by private-sector, anti-abortion health-care administrators:

> From a Lockean perspective, government can no more require one private individual to convey its moral position to another private individual than it can force individuals exercising private choices to behave in ways it deems morally correct. To do so violates those individuals' liberty as private autonomous moral agents. In addition, the forced conveyance of the government's moral position by physicians and other health care providers, backed up with legal sanctions against reluctant messengers, intrudes upon their liberty to acquire wealth and property through the exercise of a chosen legal occupation. The nonmedical aspects of informed consent forces these individuals to choose between exercising their private moral outlook in conflict with the government's officially chosen one, or continuing in their chosen profession at the cost of sacrificing their private beliefs. (Chapter 4 at 60-61)

In addition, by not extending protection to anti-abortion health-care organizations, such as Catholic hospitals, Section 2(c)(1) fails to recognize the associational liberty protecting the collective group relationships of organizations that form because of shared moral beliefs. Under a

Lockean-styled definition of liberty, "groups of individuals in a political community are free within the private sphere to 'hold and act upon [their] belief; they are even entitled to enforce their belief among members, as long as membership is genuinely voluntary' " (Bowers 1991, 6–quoting Sumner 1981, 17). In regard to this associational liberty as it applies to religion-based health-care organizations, Section 2(c)(1), in effect, fails to practice the religious tolerance toward these organizations required of it by Lockean-styled liberalism.

As underscored in Chapter 2, for Locke few things, if any, are more private and worthy of protection than religious belief because religion concerns the salvation of the soul, which is itself a task no individual can abandon to another (*A Letter concerning Toleration*, 10, 43-44). Except where the acting out of the choices concerning the salvation of the soul threatens self-preservation or brings harm to others, government has no choice but to respect and protect these choices at both the individual and group levels rather than impose its moral choices upon them. This general limitation on government applies even in those situations where private, shared religious beliefs about salvation are used to define the nature of individual or group relations toward the general community. However, like any other member of the community, government retains the opportunity to influence or entice these anti-abortion health-care administrators and organizations to behave in ways that reflect its moral choice.

Thus, to be fully consistent with the Lockean-styled perspective developed in earlier chapters, Section 2(c)(1) must be extended to protect private-sector, anti-abortion health-care administrators and organizations as well as health-care professionals involved in the actual performance of abortions. Only in this way can Section 2(c)(1) be faithful to the Lockean distinction between the public and private sphere of human existence and the limits imposed on government through this recognition.

From the above analysis, it is possible to conclude that the Freedom of Choice Act does not represent any serious or real rethinking of federal abortion policy; the constitutionally proper interpretation of a woman's liberty interest in the abortion decision; the fetal-being, its personhood, and its liberty interest in life; or the scope of government authority to balance these competing liberty claims. By failing to thoughtfully reexamine these issues, the Freedom of Choice Act cannot bring closure to the abortion debate. Indeed, any closure in the abortion debate resulting from the act likely will be temporary. Rather than closure, the passage of the Freedom of Choice Act into law likely will fan the flames of the current controversy, even while it cements a statutory pro-choice triumph.

This probable outcome is the result of the lack of attention the Freedom of Choice Act gives to balancing or blending together the two opposing positions on abortion as the Lockean-styled perspective developed in preceding chapters requires. When one reads the act, it is readily apparent that its intention is not to represent a middle position. For example, the apparent rejection of a Lockean-styled middle position is particularly evident in the euphemistic and begrudging manner in which any anti-abortion sentiment is expressed in the act. Take, for instance, the use of the euphemistic phrase "requiring a minor to involve a parent" for "parental consent" in Section 2(c)(2). A *New York Times* editorial (July 26, 1992) calls "involve" "that weasel word." The same editorial goes on to suggest, and correctly so, that this " 'weasel word' . . . needs changing to reflect candidly its sponsors' intent to let states require parental consent" (*New York Times* Editorial Board July 26, 1992, E16).

In rejecting a Lockean-styled middle position, the Freedom of Choice Act becomes little more than an attempt to replace the conservative ideological excesses of the past twelve years with liberal pro-choice excesses. That it does so is not surprising given the pro-choice majority in both the House Judiciary Committee and the Senate Labor and Human Resources Committee. Thus, the failure and inadequacy of the Freedom of Choice Act rest in its sponsors' intent to codify conventional pro-choice thinking rather than engage in any serious rethinking of a woman's liberty interest in the abortion decision, as expressed here in earlier chapters. Any resemblance to the Lockean-styled perspective developed throughout this study appears to be merely accidental.

CONCLUSION

The preceding chapters have developed and presented a Lockean-styled understanding of a woman's liberty interest in the abortion decision. This perspective defines the nature and limit of this liberty as well as the extent and means that government can regulate, restrict, and control it. In so doing, this perspective secures and balances a woman's liberty interest in the abortion decision with the viable fetal-being's interest in preservation. In the process, this perspective also defines government's role in maintaining the balance between these opposing liberty interests. It does so by showing that a constitutionally correct understanding of the liberty interest in the abortion decision requires government to be both pro-choice and anti-abortion.

The Lockean-styled perspective developed throughout the preceding chapters also presents how government is to be both pro-choice and anti-abortion. Briefly restated, this perspective dictates that government be pro-choice insofar as pro-choice means prohibiting an outright ban on pre-viability abortions or those post-viability abortions necessary to preserve the health and life of the woman involved. Also prohibited are those actions short of direct prohibition designed by government to coerce women to carry unwanted pregnancies to full term. This is the minimal pro-choice position the Constitution with its Lockean heritage requires government to follow.

The perspective developed in the preceding chapters further maintains that the Lockean-styled foundation of the Constitution also requires a minimal anti-abortion component to abortion policy. Specifically, this Lockean-styled position requires government to prohibit all post-viability abortions except those necessary to preserve the health and life of the woman. But even when an abortion is necessary to terminate a life-threatening pregnancy, this perspective still requires government to try and preserve the life of the viable fetal-being in possession of personhood.

The Constitution expects no more from abortion policy other than to encompass both these minimal pro-choice and anti-abortion requirements. Though it demands no more, it will settle for no less. Beyond these basic minimal constitutional expectations, then, government is free to be more pro-choice or anti-abortion as long as its actions are governed by the limitations specified throughout the preceding chapters. Thus, as the analysis of the Freedom of Choice Act in this chapter illustrates, if this Lockean perspective is properly followed and applied, it can serve as a blueprint or guide for constructing and evaluating proposed and existing abortion policies. By serving policy-makers in this capacity, this perspective promotes an abortion policy that is faithful to the Constitution and the original theory informing its expression of individual liberty.

But one issue remains: whether it is politically practical to expect policy-makers to behave according to the Lockean-styled perspective set out in the preceding chapters. Yes, it is. It would be naive, though, to believe that acceptance of the ideas expressed in these chapters will come easily or that the behavior of policy-makers will change in the near future. The Lockean-styled perspective presented in earlier chapters asks and expects policy-makers to replace the emotion and passions of the abortion debate with reasoned constitutional analysis, and to replace what is politically correct, safe, and expedient with what is constitutionally reasoned and correct. Thus, this perspective expects policy-makers to appreciate that abortion policy should be formulated with a clear understanding of constitutional theory—of the constitutional limits on both what government is permitted to do and the liberty individuals must have protected. If policy-makers acted accordingly and applied the Lockean-styled perspective proposed here, they would find that an abortion policy could be devised that was both pro-choice and anti-abortion, constitutionally sound, and able to at least lessen if not actually resolve the clash of absolutes that the abortion debate has become.

List of Cases

Akron v. *Akron Center for Reproductive Health*, 76 L. Ed. 2d 687 (1983)

Beal v. *Doe*, 97 S. Ct. 2366 (1977)

Bellotti v. *Baird*, 443 U.S. 622 (1979)

Bowers v. *Hardwick*, 106 S. Ct. 2841 (1986)

Doe v. *Bolton*, 93 S. Ct. 739 (1973)

Eisenstadt v. *Baird*, 405 U.S. 438 (1972)

Ginsberg v. *New York*, 390 U.S. 629 (1968)

Griswold v. *Connecticut*, 381 U.S. 479 (1968)

H. L. v. *Matheson*, 67 L. Ed. 2d 288 (1981)

Harris v. *McRae*, 100 S. Ct. 2671 (1980)

Hodgson v. *Minnesota*, 111 L. Ed. 2d 344 (1990)

Jacobson v. *Massachusetts*, 197 U.S. 11 (1905)

Lochner v. *New York*, 198 U.S. 45 (1905)

Maher v. *Roe*, 97 S. Ct. 2376 (1977)

Meyers v. *Nebraska*, 262 U.S. 390 (1923)

Ohio v. *Akron Reproductive Health Center*, 111 L. Ed. 2d 405 (1990)

Planned Parenthood of Central Missouri v. *Danforth*, 96 S. Ct. 2831 (1976)

Planned Parenthood of Kansas City, Missouri, v. *Ashcroft*, 76 L. Ed. 2d 733 (1983)

Planned Parenthood of Southeastern Pennsylvania v. *Casey*, 120 L. Ed. 2d 674 (1992)

Poe v. *Ullman*, 367 U.S. 497 (1961)

Poelker v. *Doe*, 97 S. Ct. 2391 (1977)

Prince v. *Massachusetts*, 321 U.S. 158 (1944)

Roe v. *Wade*, 93 S. Ct. 705 (1973)

Rust v. *Sullivan*, 114 L. Ed. 2d 233 (1991)

Schenk v. *United States*, 249 U.S. 47 (1919)

Simopoulos v. *Virginia*, 76 L. Ed. 2d 755 (1983)

Skinner v. *Oklahoma*, 316 U.S. 535 (1942)

Stanley v. *Georgia*, 394 U.S. 557 (1969)

Thornburgh v. *American College of Obstetricians and Gynecologists* 90 L. Ed. 2d 779 (1986)

Webster v. *Reproductive Health Services*, 106 L. Ed. 2d 410 (1989)

West Virginia State Board of Education v. *Barnette*, 319 U.S. 624 (1943)

Wisconsin v. *Yoder*, 92 S. Ct. 1542 (1972)

References

Alan Guttmacher Institute. 1991. *State Reproductive Health Monitor: Legislative Proposals and Actions* 2 (December).

——. 1990. *State Reproductive Health Monitor: Legislative Proposals and Actions* 2 (December).

Axelrod, Ruth H. 1990. Whose womb is it anyway? *Cardozo Law Review* 11: 685-711.

Baer, Judith A. 1991. Beyond rights: Fetal protection and sexual equality. Paper prepared for delivery at 1991 annual meeting of Midwest Political Science Association.

Bailyn, Bernard. 1967. *The Ideological Origins of the American Revolution*. Cambridge, MA: Harvard University Press.

Barnett, Randy E., ed. 1989. Introduction to *The Rights Retained by the People*. Fairfax, VA: George Mason University Press.

Berlin, Isaiah. 1969. *Four Essays on Liberty*. London: Oxford University Press.

Black, Charles. 1970. The unfinished business of the Warren Court. *Washington Law Review* 46: 3-32.

Boland, Reed. 1990. Recent developments in abortion laws in industrialized countries. *Law, Medicine, and Health Care* 18:404-418.

Bowers, James R., with Ummuhan Turgut. 1991. Classical Liberalism, the Constitution, and abortion policy: Can government be both pro-choice and anti-abortion? *University of Dayton Law Review* 17: 1-31.

Brest, Paul. 1990. The misconceived quest for the original understanding. In *Interpreting the Constitution: The Debate Over Original Intent*, Jack N. Rakove, ed. Boston: Northeastern University Press.

Breu, Giovanna. 1985. Words. *People*, August 12, 1985: 89-93.

Buchanan, Elizabeth. 1982. The Constitution and the anomaly of the pregnant teenager. *Arizona Law Review* 24: 553-610.

Callahan, Daniel. 1990. An ethical challenge to pro-choice advocates. *Commonwealth*, November 23, 1990: 681-687.

Callahan, Joan C. 1986. The fetus and fundamental rights. *Commonwealth*, April 11, 1986: 203-209.

Carlin, David R., Jr. 1984. Abortion and dialogue. *America*, August 24, 1984: 64.

Carlson, Margaret. 1990. Abortion's hardest cases. *Time*, July 9, 1990: 22-26.

Cohen, Carl. 1990. How not to argue about abortion. *Michigan Quarterly Review* 29: 567-583.

Congressional Quarterly Staff. 1989. Pro-choice members vow 1990 fight. *Congressional Quarterly Weekly Reports*, November 25, 1989: 3241.

Costa, Maria. 1991. *Abortion: A reference handbook*. Santa Barbara, CA: ABC-CILO.

Craig, Susan, and Dom Del Prete. 1990. The litmus test. *Empire State Report*, August 1990: 12-17.

Curry, James A., Richard B. Riley, and Richard M. Battistoni. 1989. *Constitutional Government: The American Experience*. St. Paul, MN: West Publishing Company.

Dembitz, Nanette. 1980. The Supreme Court and a minor's abortion decision. *Columbia Law Review* 80: 1251-1263.

Democrat and Chronicle Editorial Board. 1988. Civil war over abortion. *Democrat and Chronicle* (Rochester, New York), October 1988: 10A.

DeParle, Jason. 1989. Beyond the legal right. *The Washington Monthly*, April 1989: 28-44.

Diamond, Martin. 1976. The American idea of equality: The view from the founding. *The Review of Politics* 38: 313-331.

Dissent of the Pennsylvania Minority, 1787. In Ralph Ketchum, ed., *The Anti-Federalist Papers and the Constitutional Convention Debates*, 1986. New York: Mentor Books.

Donovan, Patricia. 1992. *Our Daughters' Decisions*. New York: Alan Guttmacher Institute.

Dunn, Kimberly Sharron. 1990. The prize and price of individual agency. *Duke Law Journal* 1: 81-117.

Dworetz, Steven M. 1990. *The Unvarnished Doctrine*. Durham, NC: Duke University Press.

Dworkin, Ronald. 1989. The great abortion case. *The New York Review of Books* June 29, 1989: 49-53.

Farber, Daniel A., and Suzanna Sherry. 1990. *A History of the American Constitution*. St. Paul, MN: West Publishing Company.

Feldman, Daniel Z. 1990. *The Logic of American Government*. New York: William Morrow & Company.

Fields, Martha A. 1989. Controlling the woman to protect the fetus. *Law, Medicine, and Health Care* 17: 114-129.

Foner, Eric. 1984. Introduction to *Rights of Man*, Thomas Paine. Harmondsworth, Middlesex, England: Penguin Books.

Friedman, Lawrence M. 1983. The conflict over constitutional legitimacy. In *The Abortion Dispute and the American System*, Gilbert Y. Steiner, ed. Washington, DC: The Brookings Institution.

Fuqua, David. 1980. Justice Harry A. Blackmun: The abortion decision. *Arkansas Law Review* 34: 276-296.

Glenn, Gary D. 1989. Xenophon's Hiero and "limited government." In *Politikos*, Kent Moors, ed. Pittsburgh, PA: Duquesne University Press.

———. 1979. Inalienable rights and positive government in the modern world. *The Journal of Politics* 41: 1057-1080.

———. 1975. Abortion and inalienable rights in classical liberalism. *American Journal of Jurisprudence* 20: 62-80.

Gold, Rachel Benson. 1990. *Abortion and Women's Health: A Turning Point for America?* New York: Alan Guttmacher Institute.

Goldstein, Leslie Freedman. 1981. A critique of the abortion funding decisions. *Hastings Constitutional Law Quarterly* 8:313-342.

Goldwin, Robert A. 1986. Of men and angels. In *The Moral Foundation of the American Public*, Richard H. Horowitz, ed. Charlottesville, VA: University Press of Virginia.

———. 1976. Locke's state of nature in political society. *Western Politics Quarterly* 29: 126-35.

Grisso, T., and L. Vierling. 1978. Minors' consent to treatment: A developmental perspective. *Professional Psychology* 9: 412-27.

Grobstein, Clifford. 1988. *Science and the Unborn: Choosing Human Futures*. New York: Basic Books, Inc.

Haas, Eric M. 1990. Webster, privacy and RU 486. *Journal of Contemporary Health Law and Policy* 6: 277-296.

Hartz, Louis. 1955. *The Liberal Tradition in America*. New York: Harcourt, Brace, and World, Inc.

Henkin, Louis. 1990. *The Age of Rights*. New York: Columbia University Press.

Henshaw, Stanley K. et al. 1989. *Teenage Pregnancy in the United States: The Scope of the Problem and State Responses*. New York: Alan Guttmacher Institute.

Himmelfarb, Dan. 1990. The constitutional relevance of the second sentence of the Declaration of Independence. *The Yale Law Journal* 100: 169-187.

Information Aids, Inc. 1988. *Abortion, an eternal social and moral issue*. Wiley, TX: Information Aids, Inc.

Jaffe, Harry, V. 1984. *American Conservatism and the American Founding*. Durham, NC: Carolina Academic Press.

Johnsen, Dawn. 1989. From driving to drugs. *University of Pennsylvania Law Review* 138: 179-215.

Keiter, Robert B. 1982. Privacy, children, and their parents. *Minnesota Law Review* 66: 459-518.

Kennedy, John E., and Michael Nicolazzo. 1984-85. Abortion: Toward a standard based upon clinical medical signs of life and death. *Journal of Family Law* 23: 545-563.

Ketchum, Ralph, ed. 1986. *The Anti-Federalist Papers and the Constitutional Convention Debates*. New York: Mentor Books.

Kissling, Frances. 1990. Ending the abortion war: A modest proposal. *The Christian Century*, February 21, 1990: 180-184.

Kramnick, Issac. 1987. Introduction to *The Federalist Papers*, James Madison, Alexander Hamilton, and John Jay. London: Penguin Books.

——. 1985. Editor's introduction. In *Common Sense*, Thomas Paine. Harmondsworth, Middlesex, England: Penguin Press.

Krauthammer, Charles. 1992. Pro-lifers' new battle: changing minds. *Democrat and Chronicle* (Rochester, New York), December 7, 1992: 6A.

Kuflik, Arthur. 1984. The inalienability of autonomy. *Philosophy and Public Affairs* 13: 271-298.

Lamprecht, Sterling P. 1962. *The Moral and Political Philosophy of John Locke*. New York: Russell and Russell, Inc.

Lenow, Jeffrey L. 1983. The fetus as a patient. *American Journal of Law and Medicine* 9: 1-29.

Locke, John. 1698. *Two Treatises of Government*, Peter Laslett, ed., 1988. Cambridge, England: Cambridge University Press.

——. 1691. *A Third Letter for Toleration*. In *The Collected Works of John Locke* 6, 1963. Germany: reprinted from the 1823 edition by Scientia Verlag Aalen.

——. 1690. *Some Thoughts Concerning Education*. In *The Educational Writings of John Locke*, James L. Axtell, ed., 1968. Cambridge, England: Cambridge University Press.

——. 1689. *A Letter concerning Toleration*. In *The Collected Works of John Locke* 6, 1963. Germany: reprinted from the 1823 edition by Scientia Verlag AAlen.

Losco, Joseph. 1991. Fetal rights: An examination of feminist viewpoints. Paper prepared for presentation at annual meeting of American Political Science Association.

——. 1989. Fetal abuse: An exploration of emerging philosophical, legal, and policy issues. *Western Political Quarterly* 42: 265-286.

Lutz, Donald S. 1988. *The Origins of American Constitutionalism*. Baton Rouge, LA: Louisiana State University Press.

Macedo, Stephen. 1990. *Liberal Virtues*. Oxford: Clarendon Press.

——. 1987. *The New Right v. the Constitution*. Washington DC: The Cato Institute.

Madison, James, Alexander Hamilton, and John Jay. 1788. *The Federalist Papers*, Isaac Kramnick, ed., 1987. London: Penguin Books.

Martz, Larry. 1989. The new politics rules. *Newsweek*, July 17, 1989: 21.

Mathewes-Green, Frederica. 1991. Unplanned parenthood: Easing the origin of crisis pregnancy. *Policy Review* Summer: 28-36.

✣ McDaniel, Ann. 1989. The future of abortion. *Newsweek*, July 17, 1989: 14-20.

McDonald, Forrest. 1985. *Novus Ordo Seclorum: The Intellectual Origins of the Constitution*. Lawrence, KA: University Press of Kansas.

Meilaender, Gilbert. 1989. Abortion: The right to an argument. *Hastings Center Report*, November/December: 13-16.

Melich, Tanya. 1992. Will Democrats stand up for choice? *The New York Times*, July 30, 1992: A25.

Mindle, Grant B. 1989. Liberalism, privacy, and autonomy. *The Journal of Politics* 51: 575-598.

Moore, Barbara. 1989. We'll march in D.C. for free choice. *Democrat and Chronicle* (Rochester, New York), March 27, 1989: 7A.

Morowitz, Harold J., and James S. Trefil. 1992. *The Facts of Life: Science and the Abortion Controversy*. New York: Oxford University Press.

National Issues Forum Institute. 1990. *The Battle Over Abortion*. Dubuque, IA: Kendall/Hunt Publishing Company.

O'Brien, David M. 1991. *Constitutional Law and Politics 2. Civil Rights and Civil Liberties*. New York: W. W. Norton & Company.

O'Keeffe, Janet, and James M. Jones. 1990. Easing restrictions on minors' abortion rights. *Issues in Science and Technology* Fall: 74-80.

Ostrom, Vincent. 1982. A forgotten tradition: The constitutional level of analysis. In *Missing Elements in Political Inquiry*, Judith Gillespie and Dina Zinnes, eds. Beverly Hill, CA: Sage Publications.

Paine, Thomas. 1776. *Common Sense*, Isaac Kramnick, ed., 1985. Harmondsworth, Middlesex, England: Penguin Books.

———. 1791. *Rights of Man*. New York: Penguin Books, 1985 edition.

Pangle, Thomas L. 1988. *The Spirit of Modern Republicanism: The Moral Vision of the American Founders and the Philosophy of Locke*. Chicago: University of Chicago Press.

Parry, Grant. 1978. *John Locke*. London: George Allen and Unwin.

Perry, Michael J. 1990. *Morality, Politics, and Law*. Oxford: Oxford University Press.

Petchesky, Rosalind Pollack. 1990. *Abortion and Woman's Choice: The State, Sexuality, and Reproductive Freedom*. Boston: Northeastern University Press.

Phillips, Michael. 1991. Maternal rights v. fetal rights: Court-ordered Caesareans. *Missouri Law Review* 56: 411-426.

Pollitt, Katha. 1990. A new assault on feminism. *The Nation* March 26, 1990: 409-415.

President's Commission for the Study of Ethical Problems in Medicine and Bio-medical and Behavioral Research. 1982. *Making Health Care Decisions: A Report on the Ethical and Legal Implications of Informed Consent in the Patient-Practioner Relationship* Washington, DC: Government Printing Office.

Proposed Amendments by the Virginia Convention. 1788. In *The Anti-Federalist Papers and the Constitutional Convention Debates*, Ralph Ketchum, ed., 1986. New York: Mentor Books.

Reiter, Robert C., Susan R. Johnson, and Fritz K. Beller. 1991. Abortion: Is there a rational alternative? *Obstetrics and Gynecology*, September 1991: 464-467.

Rhoden, Nancy K. 1989. A compromise on abortion? *Hastings Center Report*, July/August 1989: 32-37.

Richardson, David A. J. 1989. *The Foundation of American Constitutionalism*. New York: Oxford University Press.

———. 1980. The individual, the family, and the Constitution. *New York University Law Review* 55: 1-62.

Robertson, John A., 1983. Procreation liberty and control of conception, pregnancy, and childbirth. *Virginia Law Review* 69: 405-464.

Rodman, Hyman, Susan H. Lewis, and Saralyn B. Griffith. 1984. *The Sexual Rights of Adolescents: Competence, Vulnerability, and Parental Control*. New York: Columbia University Press.

Rosenblatt, Roger. 1992. *Life Itself: Abortion in the American Mind*. New York: Random House.

Rovner, Julie. 1992. Political Strategies Confused by *Casey*, public mood. *Congressional Quarterly Weekly Report*, August 1, 1992: 2286-2287.

———. 1992. A guide to understanding the *Casey* opinion. *Congressional Quarterly Weekly Report*, July 11, 1992: 2044-2046.

———. 1992. Abortion ruling slows momentum of freedom of choice act. *Congressional Quarterly Weekly Report*. July 4, 1992: 1951-1954.

———. 1992. Judiciary panel gets a jump on Supreme Court ruling. *Congressional Quarterly Weekly Report*, June 30, 1992: 1808.

Rubenfeld, Jed. 1991. On the legal status of the proposition that "life begins at conception." *Stanford Law Review* 43: 599-635.

Safire, William. 1989. Pro-compromise on the abortion. *Chicago Tribune*, July 8, 1989: 9.

Salholtz, Eloise. 1989. Voting in curbs and confusion. *Newsweek*, July 17, 1989: 16-20.

Samborn, Randall, 1989. The battle in the states get fiercer. *The National Law Review* December 4: 39.

Schulte, Eugene J. 1975. Tax-supported abortions: The legal issues. *Catholic Lawyer*, Winter 1975: 1-7.

Scott, Jacqueline. 1989. Conflicting beliefs about abortion: Legal approval and moral doubts. *Social Psychology Quarterly* 5: 319-326.

Shaw, Martha. 1984. Conditional Prospective Rights of the Fetus. *Journal of Legal Medicine* 5: 63-116.

Singh, Susheela. 1986. Adolescent pregnancy in the United States: An interstate analysis. *Family Planning Perspective* 18: 210-220.

Steiner, Gilbert Y., ed. 1983. Introduction to *The Abortion Dispute and the American System*. Washington, DC: The Brookings Institution. 1-12.

Stern, Nat. 1985. The Burger Court and the diminishing constitutional rights of minors. *Arizona State Law Journal* 865-904.

Storing, Herbert J. 1981. *What the Anti-Federalists Were For*. Chicago: University of Chicago Press.

Sumner, L.W. 1981. *Abortion and Moral Theory*. Princeton: Princeton University Press.

Tarcov, Nathan. 1984. *Locke's Education for Liberty*. Chicago: University of Chicago Press.

Taylor, Vincent. 1988. Columnist Cal Thomas predicts right-to-life victory in 10 years. *Democrat and Chronicle* (Rochester, New York), October 21, 1988: 1B, 3B.

Tribe, Laurence H. 1990. *Abortion: The Clash of Absolutes*. New York: W. W. Norton & Company.

—— and Michael C. Dorf. 1991. *On Reading the Constitution*. Cambridge, MA: Harvard University Press.

Trussell, James. 1988. Teenage pregnancy in the United States. *Family Planning Perspective* 20: 13-18.

United States Senate Committee and Labor and Human Resources. 1992. *The Freedom of Choice Act of 1992: Report Together With Minority Views*. Washington, DC: Government Printing Office.

The Washington Post. 1989. Bush promises 67,000 he will fight abortion. *The Democrat and Chronicle* (Rochester, New York), January 24, 1989: 1A, 10A.

Weithorn, L. A. and S. B. Campbell. 1982. The competency of children and adolescents to make informed treatment decisions. *Child Development* 53: 1589-1598.

Whitman, David. 1990. The new power of labels in the abortion wars. *U.S. News and World Report*, July 9, 1990: 20-21.

Wilkerson, Isabel. 1991. Michigan judge's views of abortion are berated. *The New York Times*, May 3, 1991: A19.

Wills, Gary. 1979. *Inventing America: Jefferson's Declaration of Independence*. New York: Vintage Press.

Yolton, John W. 1985. *Locke: An Introduction*. New York: Basil Blackwell.

Zaitchik, Alan. 1980. Viability and the morality of abortion. *Philosophy and Public Affairs* 10: 18-26.

Index

About the Author

JAMES R. BOWERS is an assistant professor of political science at St. John Fisher College in Rochester, NY. He is the author of *Regulating the Regulators: An Introduction to the Legislative Oversight of Administrative Rulemaking* (Praeger, 1990), and *American Stories: Case Studies in Politics and Government*.